014414340 Liverpool Univ

KU-571-682

THE NEW WOOD ARCHITECTURE

Acknowledgements Many people helped in the making of this book. As well as Hugh Pearman, and all the practices involved, I would like to thank Jonathan Hines of Architype and Peter Buchanan for their advice and support.

This book is dedicated to my father.

the MANCHESTER METROPOLITAN UNIVERSITY LIBRARY

First published in Great Britain in 1998

This paperback edition first published in 2001 by Laurence King Publishing an imprint of Calmann & King Ltd 71 Great Russell Street London WC1B 3BP

Copyright © text 1998 Calmann & King Ltd

All rights reserved. No part of this publication may be reproduced or transmitted in any form or by any means, electronic or mechanical, including photocopy, recording or any information storage and retrieval system, without permission in writing from the publisher.

A catalogue record for this book is available from the British Library.

ISBN 1 85669 259 0

Designed by Mark Vernon-Jones

Printed in Singapore

Photographic credits The author and the publisher would like to thank all the designers and architects involved, and the photographers whose work is reproduced. The following photographic credits are given, with page numbers in brackets: Christoph Affentranger (8, 9, 15, 16, 17, 18 top, 19); Courtesy Tadao Ando (230); Courtesy Architype (121, 122, 141 top); Ch. Bastin & J. Evrard (74, 77–83); Eilif Bjørge (147 top, 181–185); Reiner Blunck (194 bottom, 197–201); Peter Blundell-Jones (127, 128 right, 129–131); Malcolm Brown/Architectural Association (13 top); The Builder Group (156–157, 159); Chuck Choi (161, 163–167); Nev Churcher (146, 155, 156 left, 158); Nigel Corrie (104, 124–125, 139–141 bottom, 142–143); Courtesy Edward Cullinan Architects (134); Jacques Dirand (186–191); Mario Dultz, Greiner thoris! Design Gruppe, Wohnungsbaugesellschaft des Landkreises Coburg (214–224); Klaus Frahm/Contur (45–49); Geleta & Geleta Fotostudio (18 bottom); Dennis Gilbert/View (115 bottom, 116–119); Jiri Havran (75 bottom, 85–89 top); Heinrich Helfenstein (23, 25–31, 56–65); Eduard Hueber (22 bottom, 67–71); Timothy Hursley (175–179); Dieter Leistner/Architekton (105 top, 107–113); Mitsuo Matsuoka (40 bottom, 195, 231–234); Courtesy McGill University (237–239); Dr Morley/Science Photo Library (11); Shigeo Ogawa (39, 42); Ove Arup/Architectural Association (14); Max Plunger (147 bottom, 169–173, 211–215); Chris Reardon (194 top, 225–229); W. Rethmeier/Courtesy of Vogue Living (149–153); Mandy Reynolds (133, 135–137); Walter Segal/Architectural Association (13 bottom); Shinkenchiku-sha (40 top left, 41, 43, 91–95, 97, 98 right–100); Courtesy Daniel Solomon (203–209); Steko, Kesswil, Switzerland (15 left); Courtesy Thompson & Rose Architects (162 bottom); Courtesy Niels Torp (89 bottom); Ruedi Walti (22 top, 33–37, 50–55); W. Wisniewski/FLPA – Images of Nature (6–7); Harry Cory Wright (115); Courtesy Shoei Yoh Architects (75 top, 98 left, 101 right).

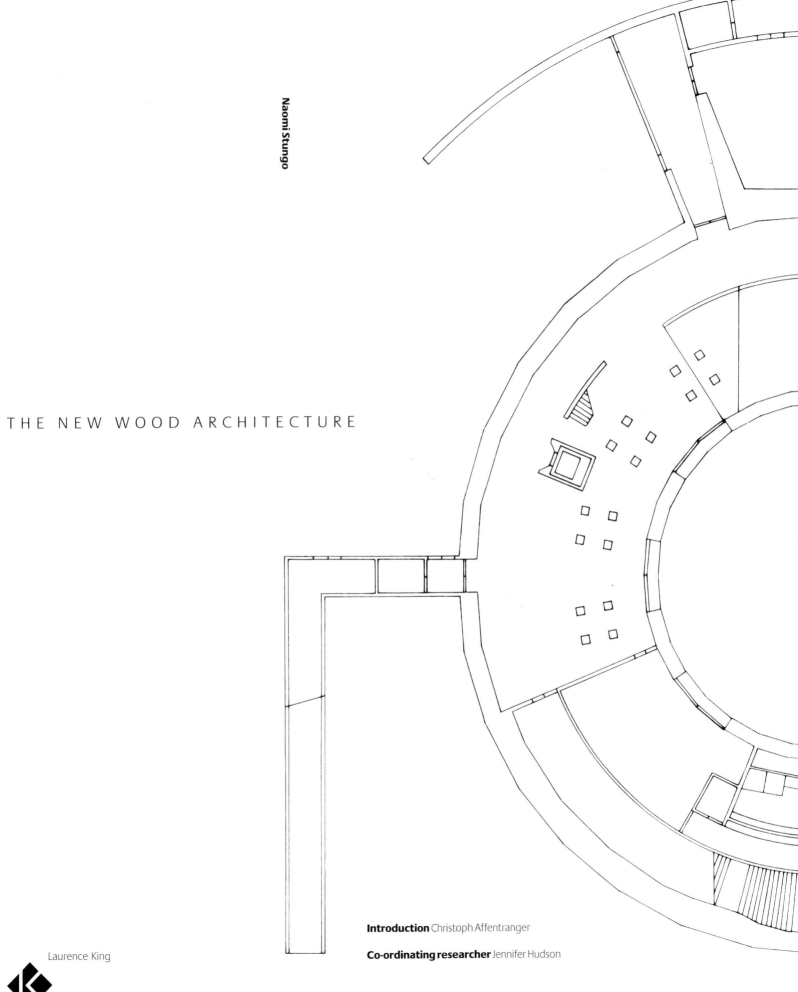

Naomi Stungo

THE NEW WOOD ARCHITECTURE

Introduction Christoph Affentranger

Co-ordinating researcher Jennifer Hudson

Laurence King

contents

chapter one

THE NEW
AESTHETIC

chapter two

STRUCTURAL
POSSIBILITIES

Trees, wood and civilization

No other plant species is so dear to humanity as the tree. It was the first, and remains the most important, of the plants used by humans, and its significance in the development of civilization cannot be underestimated. The tree has been vital in all spheres of activity: as provider of wood and fruit, as protection from the elements, and later, as a building material, as well as being an enduring symbol for the natural course of life and for constancy in an ever-changing world. The Greek historian Herodotus tells us that the great Persian king Xerxes hung golden decorations on a huge plane tree in Asia Minor in honour of its great age, and assigned one of his escorts to stand by it as guard and protector. The great ash tree, Yggdrasil, plays a central role in the mythology of the early Nordic peoples as a symbol of the world. This tree has three mighty roots: the first reaches to Nifelheim, the kingdom of the dead, the second to Jötunheim, the kingdom of the giants, and the third to Midgard, the home of humanity. This image can be found in similar form in all cultures of the world. The following quotation is from Paracelsus, one of the great European scholars of the middle ages:

'This plant ... is like a human being. It has its skin, the bark; the roots are its head and its hair; it has its distinctive shape and markings and its senses and

Wood has been one of the most popular building materials, alongside clay and stone, for thousands of years. Since the 1970s however, architects have, in general, overlooked the use of wood in favour of building with concrete, steel and synthetic materials. This book seeks to demonstrate that building with wood should be, and is, more than a passing trend instigated by a minority of architects and clients. In the present time, we are increasingly called upon to consider the ecological consequences of our actions. In the architectural world this means that we must use the raw materials at our disposal with economy and care. It was these considerations, along with innovation in the timber industry, that led to the rediscovery of building in wood – a tradition which had survived only in marginal and rural areas, and in those regions unaffected by the growing prosperity of the world's industrial nations. Wood has unique qualities as a building material it is completely recyclable and its stocks are naturally replenished, and as a source of energy it does not disturb the ecological balance of our environment. As a natural material, it is the perfect physical expression of our intimate connection with the world in which we live, at a time when this world appears to be coming increasingly virtual in character. As the examples in this book intend to demonstrate, wood architecture is the architecture of the future.

Introduction

Christoph Affentranger

1. 'The tree ... is like a human being.
It has its skin, the bark ....'
2. The forestry school in Lyss,
Switzerland, Itten & Brechbühl, 1997.

its sensitivity in the trunk. When the trunk is wounded, it dies. It has leaves, flowers and fruits as decoration, just as humans have hearing, facial features and language ... the mistletoe is its illness. Its death and dying are the season of its year."[1]

Against this background, it is scarcely surprising that even today, people will passionately defend an old tree which is threatened with the axe, especially as 500- or 1,000-year-old trees, which were once revered as gods, are now a rare sight. Over the last 500 years, greed and the over-use of natural resources, larger fields, and the construction of roads and housing estates have more or less destroyed what was once so highly honoured.

The forest, past and present

In Roman times it was said that a squirrel could travel in the forests from Toulouse to Normandy, leaping from tree to tree, without once touching the ground. Little of this ancient forest exists today. The survival or demise of trees has more to do with power and politics than we might think, as Christian Küchli has recently demonstrated.[2] Küchli shows that the much discussed present-day phenomenon of deforestation in developing countries is very similar to the processes that took place in central Europe in the early nineteenth century. At that time, industrial development was the priority for European nations. The timber from the forests was used to make sleepers for the new railways and as fuel for the growing cities. Today the forests of the developing world are mainly falling victim to slash burning, as the huge fires of the summer of 1997 in Malaysia showed only too clearly. As early as the 1950s, investigations undertaken by an international expedition in the Sahara demonstrated the connections between forest destruction, soil erosion and desert formation – and yet we have still not found an effective way to deal with the need for farmland in developing countries whose populations are expanding at an exponential rate.[3] Against this historical and economic background, it is not surprising that the countries affected are accusing northern industrialized nations of hypocrisy and unfairness, nor that the Forest Convention at the Earth Summit in Rio in 1992 failed due to an irreconcilable conflict of interests.

The forest – a vital resource for humanity

Wood is the primary source of energy for 40 per cent of the world's population; in underdeveloped areas it is often the only source of energy there is. This is all

3

too often forgotten by the developed world. In terms of quantity, this demand accounts for around half of all the wood harvested worldwide. Of the remainder, around two thirds is used for the construction industry and related areas (such as carpentry and furniture). The rest is mostly industrial wood, which serves as the raw material for producing paper, among other things. However, the significance of the world's forests lies not only in the wood they contain but, equally important, in their vital function as natural biotopes, atmospheric purifiers, sources of drinking water and habitats for a huge variety of natural species. These ecological qualities are becoming ever more highly valued in the world's industrialized regions. And yet the facts of the matter offer a stark contrast to these ecologically-minded attitudes. Today, less than 1 per cent of the total forested area of Western Europe is natural forest, and the only extensive area of primeval forest in Europe, in the Russian republic of Komi, is under immediate threat of destruction by the timber industry – from the industrialized nations, of course. The Republic of Komi is located around 1,000 kilometres (621 miles) to the north of Moscow and covers an area of around 400,000 square kilometres (154,440 square miles). Nearly two-thirds of its surface area (65 per cent) is forested, moors and marshes account for 7 per cent and only 1 per cent is used for agricultural purposes.

The world's forests in figures

According to figures from the FAO (Food and Agriculture Organization) in 1996, some 27 per cent of the earth's surface was covered with forest.[4] Eight thousand years ago there were 8.08 billion hectares (19.96 billion acres) of forest worldwide; today only 3.04 billion hectares (7.51 billion acres) remain. Europe has lost around 62 per cent of its original woodland, while the Asian-Pacific region has lost as much as 88 per cent. In its most recent studies, the World Wildlife Foundation (WWF) refers to a dramatic increase in forest destruction over the last five years. According to one study, during this period 17 million hectares (42 million acres) of primeval forest were destroyed or replaced by species-poor timber plantations. The FAO gives a figure of 11.3 million hectares (28 million acres) of forest destroyed from 1990 to 1995, although this figure refers to net loss. There is a significant difference between the two studies: the WWF study also takes into account the loss of biological diversity. For this reason, in 1997 the WWF proposed the establishment of a worldwide forest network to protect biological diversity: primeval forests should have absolute protection from human interference.[5]

In the Amazonian rainforest a tree falls every few seconds. At this rate what was once the world's largest area of primeval forest will have disappeared entirely in

3. It is not only the Brazilian rainforests that are facing annihilation. The few surviving [primeval] forests in the northern hemisphere, mainly in Russia, are threatened with the same fate.

fifty years' time. The same is also true of forests in other countries such as Costa Rica, Malaysia, Pakistan and Thailand. In percentage terms, looking at the period 1990–1995, the loss of existing forest area was largest in the Lebanon (7.8 per cent), followed by Afghanistan (6.8 per cent), the Philippines (3.5 per cent), Costa Rica (3.3 per cent), Pakistan (2.9 per cent) and Thailand (2.6 per cent). In absolute terms the losses were largest in Brazil (2.55 million hectares/6.30 million acres lost per year), followed by Indonesia (1.08 million hectares/2.66 million acres), Zaire (740,000 hectares/1,828,577 acres) and Bolivia (581,000 hectares/1,435,680 acres).

Even the few primeval forests which still survive in the northern hemisphere are becoming smaller by the year. For this reason, the forests in the growth economies of Eastern Europe and Asia – the industrial nations of the future – are especially important. Among them, attention is focused on Russia, which has the world's largest coverage of forest land (around one fifth of the world's total forested area). The future of these forests, which are mainly located in remote areas, has become increasingly uncertain since the fall of the Iron Curtain, as financially powerful timber companies from the West seek to purchase the cutting rights for relatively small sums.

Efforts made in China have shown how difficult it is to re-afforest areas once they have been deforested. Each year millions of trees are planted here, representing a huge financial investment. However, even after thirty or forty years, these new forests are not able to develop further without human intervention. Even the second generation of trees has to be planted by hand. Despite this enormous effort to counteract desert formation and to protect agricultural land, China is still heavily reliant on imports, especially because of its high consumption of firewood.

Wood certification

Historically, forests have been a vital strategic factor for rulers, with enormous significance in terms of sea voyaging and political power. They were just as important in the early industrialization of Europe, in the mining of ores and as providers of firewood to the growing cities – phenomena which can still be observed all over the world today. However, over the last two hundred years or so in Europe, people have progressed from simply using forests to caring for them and 'managing' them. The first thing Europeans had to learn was that a forest is more than just a group of trees planted together. Planting monocultures (single-species plantations), often of non-local species, leads to

4 +5. The 'woodframe construction' method, developed in North America in the mid-nineteenth century, has had a significant influence on wood architecture in the twentieth century.

4

major forest management problems which entail high levels of investment in terms of both technology and personnel. Nowadays forest managers generally try to plant mixed forests and to avoid totally deforesting large areas (which places an excessive strain on the soil and the plant and animal life of the forest). The relatively recent trend of wood certification can be seen as a reaction to global debates on forest use, biological diversity and monocultures. The world-leading system, which is becoming generally accepted, is the FSC (Forest Stewardship Council) with its four certification systems for natural forests, based on an assessment of the forest management on site. The aim of the certification is to promote sustainable forest management and to learn from previous experiences by applying a gentle pressure on the market side of the equation. Work has been in progress on developing standards for certification in the Swedish timber industry since 1996, under the auspices of the FSC. Similar developments are under way in Finland, Norway, Cameroon and Brazil. By 1998 some 9 million hectares of woodland should be certified according to FSC standards.

As well as the FSC, the Canadian Standards Organization founded the Sustainable Forest Management (SMF) project in 1994. The SMF follows the ISO 14001

environmental management system. This system solely evaluates the forest management system, and only for a particular defined area. This has the significant disadvantage that it cannot result in a product labelling system.

20th-century technological developments in wood architecture

Wood has been used as a building material for thousands of years. Throughout history, as illustrated by ancient Greek temple design, wooden buildings served as the predecessors and prototypes of architectural designs which were not carried out in stone until a much later date. The way wood grows lends itself to two fundamentally different modes of construction: strips of wood can be placed vertically, creating a roof-like structure over an open space, or it can be arranged in horizontal layers to create an enclosed area.

There is a centuries-long tradition of log construction in Europe and northern Asia. The technical limitations of this horizontal mode of construction are clearly apparent: spans which are longer than the natural length of a log create problems. Moreover, this type of construction is very wood-intensive, which makes its use practical only in the wood-rich areas of the world's temperate and polar zones such as Scandinavia, Siberia, the Balkans or the Alps.

5

6

Examples of vertical constructions can be found going back as far as the Stone Age. In areas with a restricted wood supply, the technique of arranging the wood in a 'framework' construction was perfected at an early stage: this method characteristically uses posts and bars of similar size and a storey-by-storey mode of construction. Framework construction subsequently evolved into 'post-and-beam' construction, distinguished from the framework method in that the posts and beams vary in size and thickness according to the requirements of the structure. It was the development of sawmills and sawing techniques that made possible this new form of building. Post-and-beam construction itself evolved into woodframe construction, probably the most common construction method used in the world today. This was popularized in North America in the middle of the last century, although its origins were probably in Scandinavia. In contrast to post-and-beam construction, where the beams are put in place on site, one by one, in woodframe construction the walls and ceilings are assembled as complete units on the ground before being erected. Frame construction typically displays standardized wood posts and crossbars, packed closely together, with diagonally arranged roofboards and chipboard and gypsum panels for reinforcement.

6. Multihalle at the National Garden
Exhibition in Mannheim (1974). Frei
Otto in collaboration with Carlfried
Mutschler.

7 + 8. The Steko wood construction method developed by Swiss company Steko in Kesswil is one of many examples of the highly innovative character of the timber industry today. Steko modules are wooden units, similar to traditional bricks in terms of size and handling. This system opens up the sphere of wood architecture to those who are not familiar with traditional wood construction methods. The Steko wood building system is being patented in all the world's major markets and the trademark is protected by law.

Spans and steel

The most spectacular development in wood construction in the twentieth century was the invention of glued-laminated timber (or girders consisting of pieces of wood stuck together in various ways) which represented a huge advance in terms of bridging wide spans. New connecting methods, especially the nailboard method, developed in the USA, brought about improvements in the assembly of individual pieces of wood and led to the development of new types of joint with better load-bearing capabilities. The construction of wide-spanned halls would not be possible without steel joints. However, steel is not only used for joints: it can also be used to reinforce wood, in the same way as it is used with concrete.

The second method of bridging large spans with wood consists in joining together thin slats to form an area-covering structural element. However, this type of construction has still not become widely established, perhaps because wide-spanning elements are much more difficult to calculate than simple beams. German architect and engineer Frei Otto has made significant advances in this area, for example with the Multihalle on the site of the National Garden Exhibition in Mannheim, produced in collaboration with Carlfried Mutschler. In years to come it is likely that new computer-based simulation systems will lead to innovations in both area-covering structural elements and shell construction.

From the beam to the panel: new semi-finished products

Recently, trends have developed alongside the established construction techniques, which are all based on the natural rod-like shape of wood. These trends are based on the desire to standardize wood as a material, ironing out its variable characteristics (such as its expansion and contraction and its non-uniformity of structure) in order to simplify the business of calculating and handling. This trend, which could be dubbed 'homogenization', is not a new thing in itself. In ancient Egypt there were attempts to modify the characteristics of wood by cutting it into very thin panels which were glued together crosswise or on to a solid support material. For centuries this method was used only for marquetry and furniture. It was not until the development of large-scale plywood boards, as Thomas Baggenstos and Christian Cerliani have demonstrated, that the panel construction method opened up a new dimension for wood building.[6] Now the range of glued panels on offer has expanded considerably, encompassing new types of chipboard and parti-

7

8

9

cleboard. Another advantage of this type of system, as compared to traditional building woods, is that lower-quality wood can also be used in the production of the panels.

With the panel construction method, the load is borne not by individual posts but by whole panels, which only need to be reinforced against buckling. Wood can withstand very large pressures and so these panels only have to be a few centimetres thick in order to bear the load of a whole house. However, the panels have to be prefabricated in specialist workshops.

The search for a new form

At the present time in Europe there is a great deal of interest in using wood in the construction of multi-storey buildings: experimental buildings have been built in Finland, Sweden, Southern Germany and Switzerland. Driven by the economic interests of the timber industry, some significant restrictions in wood construction, primarily relating to fire protection, have been partially lifted or reinterpreted in recent years. It remains to be seen how far the market will make use of the new possibilities this opens up. However, the industry is anticipating two-figure growth rates in the years ahead in central and northern Europe.

9. Corner detail of the forestry school in Lyss, Switzerland, showing the external structure of the façade. The school was produced by the architects Itten & Brechbühl in 1997. Thirty-four 15 metre (49 ⅓ feet) high silver firs form the load-bearing pillars of the three-storey building. The floors are also made of wood, as are the façades and the staircases.

10. The experimental house Villa
Vision in Høje Tastrup, Denmark,
was built on the site of the Dansk
Teknologisk Institut in 1995, with the
intention of bringing together in a
single structure the latest scientific
discoveries regarding construction,
energy and the environment. As well
as solar collectors and a low-energy
design, the house also features
water recycling and the latest
communications technologies.

10

11. The buildings designed by the young Swiss architect Gion A. Caminada exemplify the works of a new generation of architects, who are looking not to create a contrast between historical sites and new buildings, but rather to forge links between the old and the new. This multipurpose hall in Vrin (1997), in the Swiss canton of Graubünden, is the extension of a school building.

12. The architectural language of Hungarian Imre Makovecz represents an attempt to create a national identity. His works can be seen as a continuation of National Romanticism, a movement which predominated in the Scandinavian region in the early twentieth century. This is the church in Paks, Hungary, 1987.

11

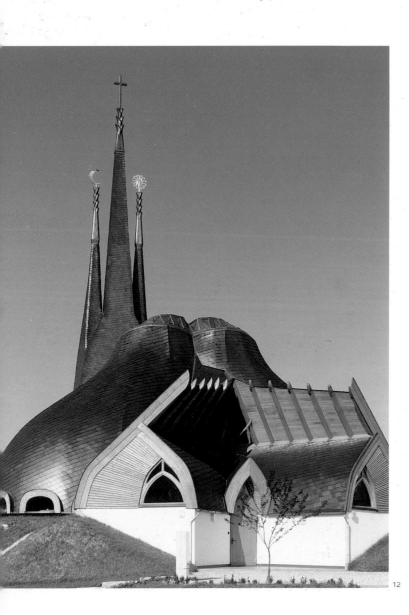

12

Alongside these technological developments, contemporary architects are exploring a new design world with wood architecture. In many cases, we can see traditional wood construction methods and typologies returning, in new forms made possible by technological advances. Traditional wood building methods are generating increased interest and are set to grow in importance. Another interesting trend is the development of a wood-based architecture which originated with the anthroposophic movement: new and surprising possibilities are constantly emerging here, in works like those of Swedish architect Assmussen. On the technical side, the current challenges are to reduce energy consumption in both the construction and the operation of buildings, particularly in temperate and cold regions of the globe. No-energy and low-energy houses and sustainable buildings are just a few of the innovations that are forcing their way to the forefront of design. Thanks to their ecological advantages, their outstanding capacity for natural air conditioning and their excellent ability to insulate, wooden buildings will clearly have a large part to play in these trends. There is no reason, therefore, to regard the current interest in building with wood as just a passing phase, in fact it is quite the reverse: wood architecture is here to stay.

13. The combination of glue and wood has led to some significant innovations in wood construction methods in this century. Here are the pillars, some 20 metres (65 ¾ feet) high, of the roof over the ruins of the castle at Koldinghus, Denmark (architects: Inger og Johannes Exner, 1995).

Footnotes

1 Quotation in Köstler, Josef, *Offenbarung des Waldes*, Verlag F. Bruckmann, Munich, 1941.

2 Küchli, Christian, *Wälder der Hoffnung*, Buchverlag NZZ, Zurich, 1997. English version published by Earthscan, London, 1997.

3 Kollmannsperger, Franz, *Drohende Wüste – Erlebnisse und Ergebnis der internationalen Sahara Expedition 1953–54*, Brockhaus, Wiesbaden, 1957.

4 Figures from FAO study of March 1997.

5 *Neue Zürcher Zeitung*, 9.10.97.

6 Baggenstos, Thomas and Cerliani, Christian, *Sperrholzarchitektur*, Baufachverlag AG, Dietikon, 1997.

chapter one

Designed almost exclusively by young, forward-looking architects, these structures pre-

sent a new vocabulary for timber buildings. United by their attention to formal simplicity,

they reverberate with the pared down visions of early modernism. Concurrently, their

fundamental modernity is flaunted through subtle games-playing and an exploration into

1

In a school playground in the Swiss city of Basle stands an unpainted building, stark and plain save for its slatted timber sides and rhythmically placed windows. From here we move to Berg, in Germany, where on the outskirts of the city can be found a striking wooden house, its horizontally clad walls contrasting with huge vertical shutters in a highly abstract composition. In a snowy field in Lustenau, Austria, there is a kindergarten, again unadorned except for its bold red and white paintwork and the patterns created by its windows. These are different countries and different building types. But linking them, and the other buildings in this chapter, is the fact that they are designed almost exclusively by a new generation of young, avant-garde architects. (The exception is the Museum of Wood by Tadao Ando, who is rather older.) And all are built out of wood.

Rejecting the machine aesthetic of the high-tech movement and the overblown flamboyance of deconstructivism, this new generation is reassessing the legacy of modernism. For some, like the Swiss practice of Burkhalter & Sumi, this is a conscious activity (the partners have made in-depth studies of early twentieth-century architects such as Jean Prouvé and Carlo Mollino). For others, it seems to happen at a more subconscious level. Either way these buildings carry something of the spirit of earlier twentieth-century greats, particularly in the frequent use of prefabricated elements and in their pared down aesthetics. Frank Lloyd Wright, whose Usonian houses were based on a kit of parts developed around the size of a standard sheet of plywood, is there; so too is Walter Gropius (who, apart from designing several wooden buildings also co-developed the prefabricated 'general panel system'); Mies van der Rohe (who in his essay on architectural education wrote 'Where does the structure of a house or building appear with greater clarity than in the wooden buildings of the ancients...?'); Arne Jacobsen. The list goes on.

And yet it would be wrong to think that this young generation has simply picked up the modernist baton. There are significant differences between their work and that of their mentors. Perhaps the most striking is the way that 'legibility' – the idea that a building should reveal its construction and all, on first glance – is not an issue for most of the architects. Tricks are played: concrete- and timber-framed elements are clad identically so it is unclear which is which; roofs are not supported in the way one might think they are, and so on.

The second vital influence, which goes some way towards explaining why so much of this work is happening in the Swiss-German-Austrian belt of central

2

Europe, is the minimalist style of the Basle-based practice of Herzog & de Meuron. Several of the architects from this new generation worked there before setting up practices of their own, while most of the others clearly admire the practice's work, particularly in its emphasis on the essence of materials. The rough-hewn, plain planking – timber in its virgin state – used to clad so many of the buildings shown over the coming pages is highly reminiscent of the way Herzog & de Meuron 'play up' materials in their buildings. So, too, is the way both horizontal and vertical timber cladding is frequently used on different surfaces of the same building, another device that reinforces the physicality of the skin.

The influence of Herzog & de Meuron is more than just skin deep, however. The buildings shown on the following pages, with their highly abstract, geometrical forms stripped of superfluous detailing, also pay homage to the practice's minimal aesthetic. But again there are differences. Whereas Herzog & de Meuron's buildings can seem chilly, almost too distilled, the projects included here glow with warmth and light. This is partly due to the material – wood is naturally sensuous and appealing – but it is also a result of the way it is handled. Whether brightly painted or left plain, these buildings have an inviting quality that makes them popular with users and neighbours alike.

3

1. Family house, Steinmann & Schmid.
2. Showroom and warehouse,
Baumschlager & Eberle.
3. Forestry outpost, Marianne
Burkhalter & Christian Sumi.

1. Site plan.
2. Corridor leading into one of three playrooms.

familiar environment of the home to the unknown world beyond. Indeed, the way the building is conceived – as a play of 'positive' and 'receding' volumes – is reminiscent of a children's game. The two main elements (the kindergarten and infant/apartments block) are created from simple cubes painted red or white. Fenestration on both parts is limited to two types of window (horizontal 'fenêtre longue' windows or vertical French doors), which are used in a variety of ways across the elevations. The building was constructed in a straightforward way. Like many of Burkhalter & Sumi's buildings, and many of the early twentieth-century buildings the practice so admires, the kindergarten is built from prefabricated timber frames. These have been clad with tongue-and-groove rain-screen wood cladding (either vertical or horizontal), plus a windproof paper and 140mm (5 ½ inches) of insulation. The ceiling plates are made from solid wood planks. So, too, is the flat roof, which consists of laminated timber beams protected by 120mm (4 ¾ inches) of insulation and covered in a layer of tar and pebbles. Inside, a birch plywood skin (birch is a local timber) lines the rooms which, together with windows at both adult- and child-height, helps the interior spaces glow warm and light. A dramatic bicycle shed completes the composition; this is again made from prefabricated panels but with horizontal strips of construction-site 'keep out' tape around its sides – a further play on the idea of construction and building.

Burkhalter & Sumi is a young Zurich-based practice that specializes in timber buildings. Most of their buildings are built either entirely of wood or of timber and concrete. This has been the case right from the early days, when they built small country houses, through to their current portfolio of hotels, schools and municipal buildings. Perhaps this love of wood is related to the fact that Sumi's father was a cabinet maker; looking at the practice's confident and refined detailing, you can certainly imagine that skilled carpentry is an influence. As important an influence, however, is early twentieth-century timber architecture. Fascinated by 'the intelligence of their constructional conception as well as their regional adaptability', Marianne Burkhalter and Christian Sumi have made careful studies of a number of the classic timber buildings, including Frank Lloyd Wright's Usonian houses, timber structures by Jean Prouvé and Carlo Mollino, and wood houses by Arne Jacobsen and Mies van der Rohe. One of the practice's most striking buildings is a kindergarten in the west Austrian town of Lustenau. An annexe running diagonally off the main kindergarten building provides additional space for an infants' care centre at ground-floor level, with three one-bedroom apartments on the first floor. The building has all the crisp detailing and pared-down geometry of Burkhalter & Sumi at its best. With its bright primary colours and child-friendly details, it is a delightful space for children making the transition from the

1

Kindergarten

Lustenau, Austria, 1992–94

Marianne Burkhalter

& Christian Sumi

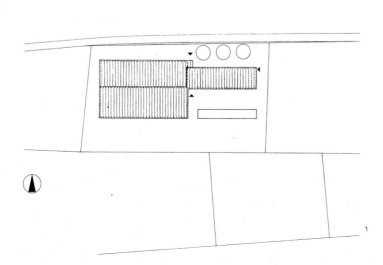

1

3

Kindergarten

3. South elevation.
4. Ground-floor plan.

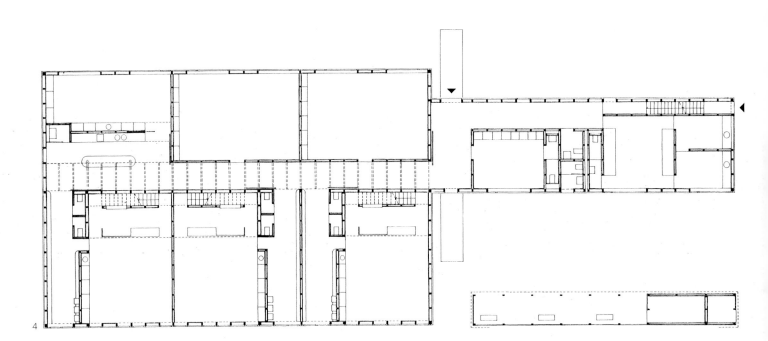

4

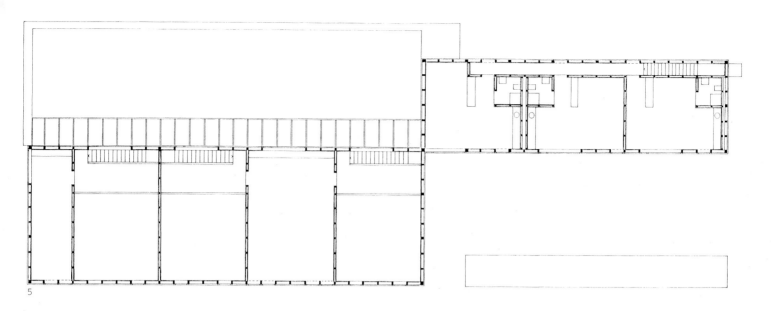

5

Kindergarten
5. First-floor plan.
6. North elevation.

following pages
7. South elevation.

6

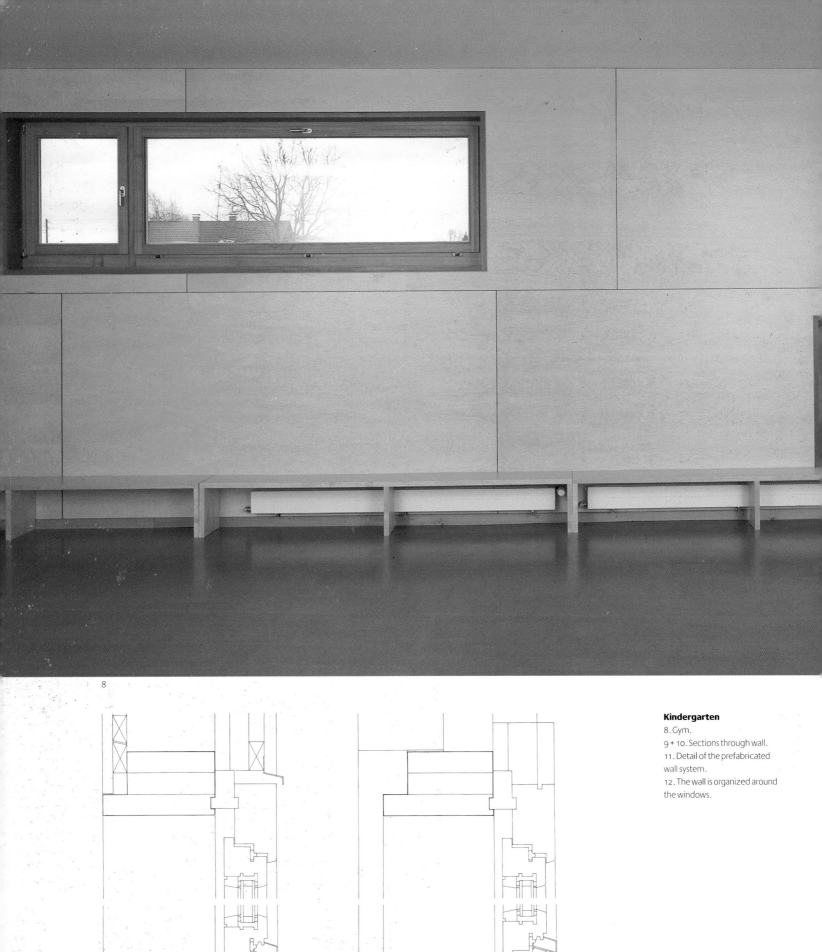

8

Kindergarten

8. Gym.

9 + 10. Sections through wall.

11. Detail of the prefabricated wall system.

12. The wall is organized around the windows.

9

10

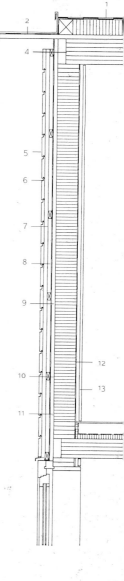

key

roof
1 tar layer with small pebbles, 3mm
2 EGV tar layer, 1mm
3 insulation, 120mm
4 laminated wooden supporting
   beam, 160mm

wall
5 planed wooden façade, 19mm
6 horizontal wooden ventilation
   slats, 25mm
7 vertical wooden ventilation slats,
   25mm
8 windproof paper
9 waterproof chipboard, 24mm
10 Flumroc insulation, 140mm
11 damp-proof layer
12 wooden slats, 20mm
13 birch plywood, 18mm

Kindergarten
Architect: Marianne Burkhalter and
Christian Sumi, Zurich, Andrea Bassi
Engineer: Ingo Gehrer, Höchst
Landscape gardener: Stöckli, Kienast
and Köppel, Zurich, Günther Vogt

12

1. Site plan.
2. Corner detail.

large pieces. Steinmann & Schmid describe their architecture as a rational response to problems but, of course, there is more to it than that. With its pitched roof and timber façades, the house can also be seen as a game: a take on the traditional Swiss chalet. But where chalets are decorated and brightly painted, Steinmann & Schmid's house is stark and plain. And instead of bursting open to the landscape with extrovert balconies and terraces, their house recedes into itself, the windows set back in the main façades and blanked out by sliding shutters. Games are also played inside the house, where large architectural elements designed like pieces of furniture organize the layout of the main living spaces and provide huge amounts of storage space. The entrance hall is separated from the living area by a partition wall that on closer inspection turns out to be a continuous bank of cupboards (some open on to the hall, others on to the living space). The main living area is a large, low-ceilinged volume with built-in bookcases running along most of one wall. Besides this, the main element is the kitchen which stands like a self-contained island in the middle of the plan, dividing the living area on one side from the dining space on the other. Upstairs, three bedrooms and a bathroom open off the landing. A fourth bedroom can be created by pulling a partition across an open-plan space.

Architects and furniture designers Peter Steinmann and Herbert Schmid are among the youngest architects featured in this book. Still only in their 30s, they set up their Basle-based practice in 1992. Like the minimal tables, chairs and storage systems that they design, their architecture is rigorous and pared down in style. 'Our buildings grow out of scrupulous analysis of the site,' they say. 'Their design is defined as much by spatial considerations as by the needs of users. Spatial and visual interest is generated through economic use of materials, forms and colours.' This is clearly demonstrated in the timber single-family house that they have designed on the outskirts of Berg, in the Canton of Thurgau. The two-storey house has an awkward location, wedged between an agricultural zone and a main railway line. Making the most of the site, Steinmann & Schmid have created a compact house that turns its shortest elevation towards the railway lines and opens up to face the flat countryside with windows down most of its length. Being largely prefabricated, the house took just 20 weeks to erect. Once the timber floor deck was in place, exterior walls made of 16cm (6 ¼ inch) thick timber, lagged with insulation, were lifted into place by crane. On the exterior, the timbers were clad with horizontal lapped boards of untreated larch. The roof was also factory-made (with the exception of the battens and the joists), and was assembled on site from four

2

Family house

Berg, Switzerland, 1994

Steinmann & Schmid

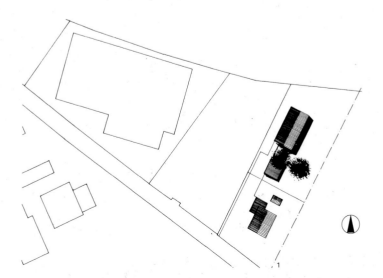

3

4

Family house
3. Rear and side elevations.
4. Prefabricated elements being craned into place.
5. Junction of the horizontally clad timber walls and vertical wooden shutters.

5

7

Family house
6. Partially obscured window.
7. Window detail.
8. House with shutters drawn.

6

8

9

Family house
9. The dining room.
10. Living room with built-in
bookcases.
11. View towards the kitchen.
12. First-floor plan.
13. Ground-floor plan.

10

11

9

4   10   4   4   4

12

Family house
Architect: Steinmann & Schmid, Basle

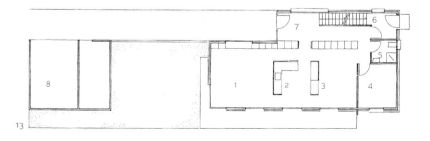

7   6

5

8   1   2   3   4

13

key
1 living
2 kitchen
3 dining
4 bedroom
5 shower/wc
6 entrance (garden side)
7 main entrance
8 garage
9 office
10 bathroom

1. Site plan.
2. View from inside the inner courtyard.

between this outer skin and an inner void, 22 metres (72 feet) in diameter, is a ring of exhibition space. The construction is not wholly of timber. The museum sits on a concrete framework which creates a level base across the sloping site. Huge steel portals bedded into the concrete provide the building's rigidity. These structural elements are entirely covered by the Douglas fir cladding which comes down right to the ground. This gives the building its all-timber appearance, an effect which is reinforced by a series of timber post and beams inside. Visitors reach the museum via a long ramping pathway that slices along the forest's contour lines, pierces the building's outer skin and leads into the exhibition area. This is a dramatic space, punctuated at regular intervals by groups of four 18 metre (60 foot) laminated cedar columns that rise up to support clusters of cedar beams. Although purely decorative, the post-and-beam construction evokes traditional Japanese building techniques. Short flights of steps, terraces and gentle slopes vary the experience of walking around the exhibition space and provide a number of different display areas. Although the space is windowless (with the only daylight entering through small roof lights), views out to the landscape are provided by an inclined bridge which penetrates the building, crossing the void and leading to an annexe which has spectacular views of the unspoilt forest all around.

Since rising to international prominence in the 1980s with a string of highly abstract structures, Tadao Ando has been associated in most architects' minds with beautifully detailed, bare-faced concrete buildings. But this is not the only material in which he builds. In the early 1990s Ando was commissioned to design the Japanese pavilion at Expo '92 in Seville (see pages 230–235) and began experimenting with timber construction. The Museum of Wood is one of three largely timber buildings he has designed since then. The building was commissioned by the Hyogo prefectural government which wanted a building to celebrate the 45th anniversary of National Arbor Day – an annual tree-planting event started in the 1950s as part of the post-war effort to restore the Japanese countryside. Its brief to Ando was that the building should be made of wood and provide display spaces for exhibitions about trees and timber products. The Museum of Wood is sited deep in forests in the north-west corner of Hyogo, an area known for its cedar trees and good-quality timber products. Ando felt that the museum should appear to grow naturally from its site within the enclosing trees, merging, over time, with its surroundings. For this reason, the building is doughnut-shaped in plan with an open inner courtyard or void. Its blank outer drum is 46 metres (150 feet) in diameter and clad in horizontal boards of Douglas fir, which will weather to a silvery grey. Sandwiched

3

Museum of Wood

Mikata-gun, Hyogo,

Japan, 1994

Tadao Ando Architect

& Associates

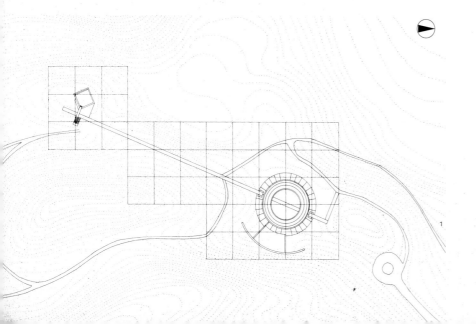

3

Museum of Wood

3. The ramp along which visitors approach the building slices right through the museum, ensuring views through to the forest beyond.
4. Aerial view showing the building's doughnut-shaped plan and the approach through the forest.
5. One of the project's main objectives was to preserve the area's historic forests.

4

5

Museum of Wood

6. View of one of the main exhibition spaces sandwiched between the building's inner and outer skins.
7. Although not structural, the post-and-beam construction dramatically illustrates traditional wood building techniques.
8. Plan and section superimposed.

6

7

Museum of Wood
Project team: Tadao Ando Architect &
Associates

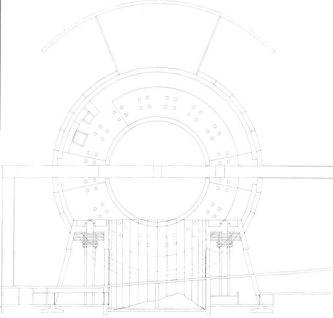

8

1. Long elevation showing the double-height house and single-storey studio.
2. Detail of the studio in the foreground with the house behind.

Solid laminated columns (of the same dimensions as the hollow beams), their joints reinforced with steel finger plates and bolts, define the corners of the building where it changes height or width. They also give the building stability. The studio's long walls were otherwise made from the hollow beam system, clad with red cedar, while its short walls are finished with full-height metal-frame windows. The roof, which is made from the same beam structure, has a projecting sloping cornice made of 10mm (⅜ inch) thick aluminium. This helps protect the untreated timbers and prevents rain getting inside on wet days when the windows are left open. The small house, which is used mainly as a guest wing, is a far simpler piece of design. Set into a trench (unlike the studio, which is raised above the ground on a wood deck), the two-storey building is a 7.2x7.2 metre (23 ½ x 23 ½ foot) box. It uses the same box-beam structure as the studio, this time with large shuttered windows down one side, and roof lights. With its minimal detailing and pure abstracted forms, the Bangert house and studio is very much at the forefront of contemporary timber design, using wood in ways that have hitherto only been possible with steel or concrete. This has largely been possible due to the ingenuity of the engineers for the project, Ingenieurgruppe Flösser (who also work with other cutting-edge architects such as Herzog & de Meuron and Peter Zumthor), who played a key part in helping develop the timber system.

The Bangert house and studio is the first house that Dieter Thiel has designed. Thiel, who is a product and exhibition designer as well as an architect, worked with Fiat, Mario Bellini and Philippe Starck among others before setting up his own practice. Thiel was commissioned by the publisher, Albrecht Bangert, to design a house and studio on a beautiful site in the southern Black Forest, near the Swiss border. Thiel chose to design the two elements of the project as two separate buildings – a large single-storey studio and a smaller two-storey house – both of which are set some distance from a 1950s house with which they share the site. Both new buildings use the same construction method: a proprietary system of prefabricated laminated beams that allows for a completely seam-free, highly abstract finish. The system uses hollow composite beams measuring 20x30 cm (7 ¾ x 11 ¾ inches) in cross-section, placed together in a tongue-and-groove system to form a continuous wall. It is a very direct building method, rather like designing a modern-day log cabin. The outer layer of the wall becomes the building's external skin, and the inner layer its internal lining. Insulation inside the hollow cavity, and wool fibre between the beams, keeps the structure warm and dry. The main studio building consists of three differently sized volumes or 'boxes'. Together these form a continuous open-plan building, 17.6 metres (58 ¾ feet) in length, which nevertheless has three different ceiling heights and three widths.

4

House and office

Schopfheim, Germany, 1996

Dieter Thiel

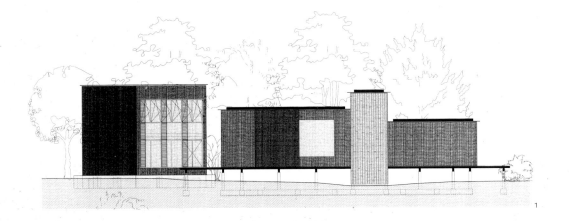

1

3

House and office
3. Long elevation.
4. Ground-floor plan of both buildings.

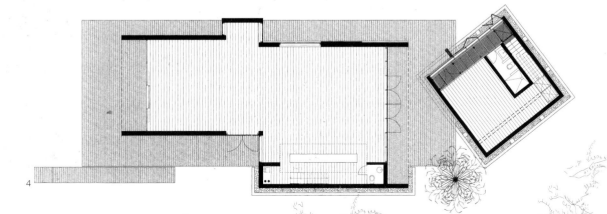

4

5

House and office

5. Double-height shutters ensure privacy in the house.
6. Corner detail showing how box beams are connected.
7. Cross-section through hollow box beam.
8. Short elevation with the studio in the foreground and house behind.

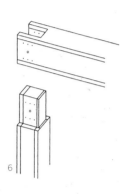

6

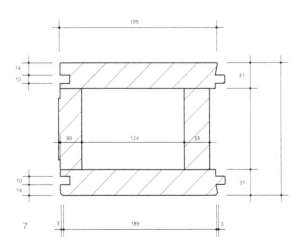

7

8

9

10

House and office
9. Inside the studio.
10. View from the studio looking towards the house.
11. Short section through the house.
12. First-floor level in the house.

House and office

Architect: Dieter Thiel, Basle
Structural engineer: Ingenieurgruppe
Flösser, Hermann Müller-Bornemann,
Bernhard Strasser, Bad Säckingen,
Germany
Woodwork: A.J. Kunzweiler, Weil
am Rhein
'Lignatur' elements: Lignatur AG,
Waldstaat/Laufenburg

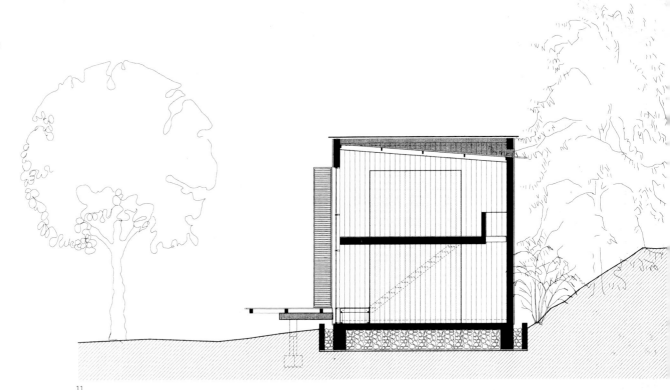

11

12

1. South elevation.
2. Corner detail under the roof on the
front elevation.

ing patterns and shadows along its walls. But the main source of daylight is the end wall where the pine planking is replaced by fully-glazed French windows which can be flung open to reach a small balcony. Inside, in keeping with its simple, crate-like exterior form, the kindergarten consists of one large play space with a small entrance lobby, toilet and kitchen area. These spaces, lined in sheets of plywood, have been polished with beeswax until they glow soft and smooth. Well-considered child-focused details enliven the otherwise plain main room. The lower tier of windows provides a series of perfect peep-holes on to the outside world. Little perches built on to the lower part of the French windows create child-height seats that form either a single line when the windows are pulled shut, or pairs of facing seats when they are thrown open. Fittingly, the kindergarten is a highly didactic piece of construction where each element can be read and its purpose understood. The floor joists are clearly visible, projecting out beneath the building. Similarly, the outer planking is simply a protective layer: a decorative but not weatherproof finish through which one can see into the inner workings of the walls.

Morger & Degelo's work has a paradoxical quality shared by many of the projects shown in this chapter. The young Basle-based practice often builds in wood, leaving the timber rough and natural-looking. And yet, expressing themselves through construction details, their stark, angular buildings have a highly abstract, man-made quality. One of the most striking examples of this contrary combination is a kindergarten they designed in Basle. The building is a temporary play centre, set within the grounds, but independent from, a large nineteenth-century school in the city centre. Clad on three sides in horizontal planks of untreated pine, Morger & Delego's kindergarten sits in the playground like a huge crate, which evokes a kind of man-made nature. Made from prefabricated panels, the rectangular box is raised above the ground on two concrete beams and lined on the inside with plywood. A layer of insulation between the inner and outer skins – itself protected from rain by sheets of roofing felt – keeps inside temperatures comfortable, while vertical frames in the wall joints link the roof and floor and help to counteract wind loads. The plywood ceiling and roof deck act together as a rafter to form a stiff roof plate that spans the internal space and carries roof and the weight of snow. Two rows of small windows – one at a child's height, the other at an adult's – along each of the long elevations bring daylight into the building, cast-

5

Kindergarten

Basle, Switzerland, 1989

Morger & Degelo Architekten

3

4

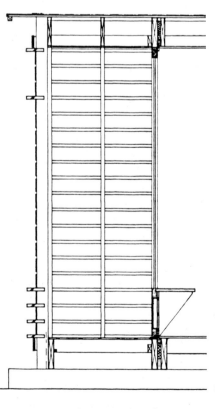

5

Kindergarten

3. South elevation. The kindergarten appears to be starkly man-made and horizontal in contrast to the surrounding trees.

4. Detail of the prefabricated panel system showing the horizontal pine cladding.

5. Detail showing the window seating system.

6. Short section.

7. Rear elevation. French doors open out on to a small verandah.

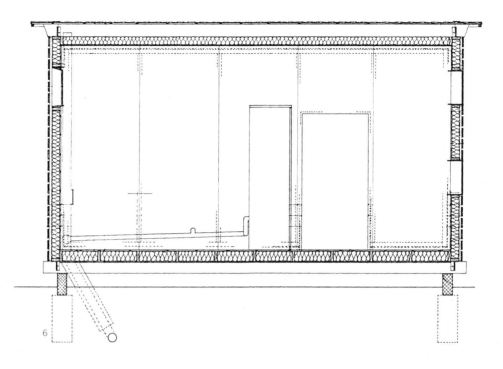

6

7

Kindergarten

8. Inside, the main kindergarten area is a single volume with child- and adult-height windows.

9. Plan.

10. The building is tightly crafted. The French doors double up to provide pairs of facing benches.

8

Kindergarten

Architect: Morger & Degelo und Prêtre

Project team: Morger & Degelo und Prêtre

Structural engineer: Weiss-Guitlod-Gisi

Quantity surveyor: Morger & Degelo und Prêtre

Woodwork: Jean Cron AG

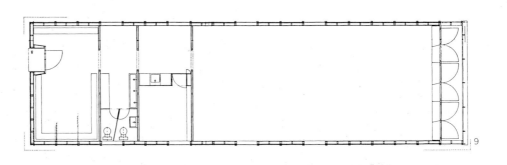

9

1. Turbenthal, west elevation.
2. Rheinau, north elevation.
3. Turbenthal, shed with steel props.

which has to take heavy machinery, is made of concrete. The shed, meanwhile, is of timber construction with six 6 metre (19 ½ foot) unfinished tree trunks as posts. Its roof is treated as an abstract plane: box beams form composite trusses, with steel props and tension ties projecting beneath, so that it appears to float, de-materialized, above the posts. The administration building is also of timber construction, with a roof of insulated box beams. Its timber frame is clad with a vapour-penetrable windbreak rather than the more usual particle board (which contains toxic formaldehyde). The building's interior is clad in fir plywood. Like the window frames, oak flooring and built-in furniture, the interior cladding is simply finished in beeswax. At the Rheinau forestry station, the three 'building blocks' are laid out so as to give definition to the edge of a pre-existing glade. The administration building and garage are grouped together in a single block which sits a little distance from the shed, creating a courtyard-like exterior space between the buildings. Colour is used to dramatic effect, differentiating the red, horizontally clad administration area from the garage with its vertical, naturally finished boarding. As at Turbenthal, there is a mix of wood and concrete construction which is not immediately apparent to the casual observer. At Rheinau, the interior cladding is of untreated pine boards with an oak trim.

Burkhalter & Sumi's kindergarten at Lustenau (see pages 24–31) may look like a giant set of toys, but it is the practice's forestry outposts, with their brightly coloured components arranged in different configurations, that really work like building blocks. In 1991 the building department of the canton of Zurich asked the practice to design a kit-of-parts system of forestry outposts to house offices and equipment stores for the foresters who manage the woods around Zurich. The system had to be flexible enough to be built on a number of very different sites throughout the region. Since the early 1990s a number of the outposts have been completed, two of which are shown here. The kit consists of three elements or 'building blocks': an administration building, a garage and an open-sided shed (in effect little more than a roofed-over open space). In a woodland clearing at Turbenthal, the three elements are grouped into two blocks and wedged into the contours of the land. The larger garage/shed block fronts the site, while the smaller administration wing sits behind and slightly to one side of it. The two groups of buildings form a striking pair, their roofs at different angles, heightening the abstract composition of the whole. The larger of the two blocks – the garage/shed unit – is treated as a single entity, with continuous red-painted planks running down its length, despite the fact that its component parts were built very differently. The garage,

6

Two forestry outposts

Turbenthal, Switzerland

1991–93

Rheinau, Switzerland

1992–94

Marianne Burkhalter

& Christian Sumi

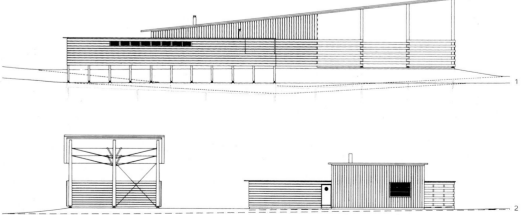

Turbenthal forestry outpost
4. Site plan.
5. View with the shed in the
foreground and the administration
block behind and to one side.
6. Plan.
7. Long section.

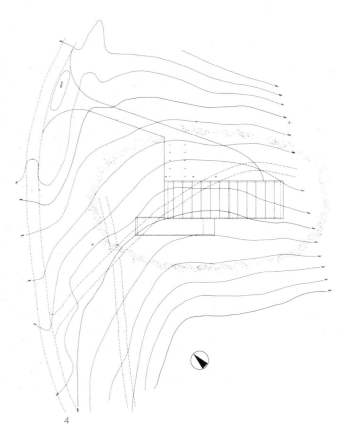

4

5

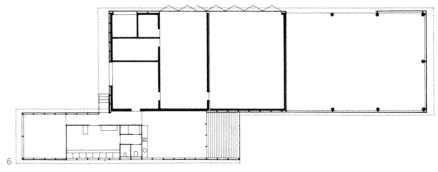

6

7

8

Turbenthal forestry outpost
8. The interior is lined in fir plywood.
9. The shed and, behind, the trees it so closely resembles.
10. Detail of the north elevation. Colour changes differentiate the garage from the administration building.
11. Section through a wall.

key
1 tar with small pebbles, 3mm
2 EGV tar layer, 1mm
3 insulation, 50mm
4 hollow beam construction insulation
5 damp-proof layer
6 two sheets plasterboard, 36mm
7 rough-sawn wooden façade, 21mm
8 ventilation slats, 40mm
9 windproof paper
10 beam structure, 120mm
11 Flumroc insulation, 120mm
12 damp-proof layer
13 plywood, 18mm

9

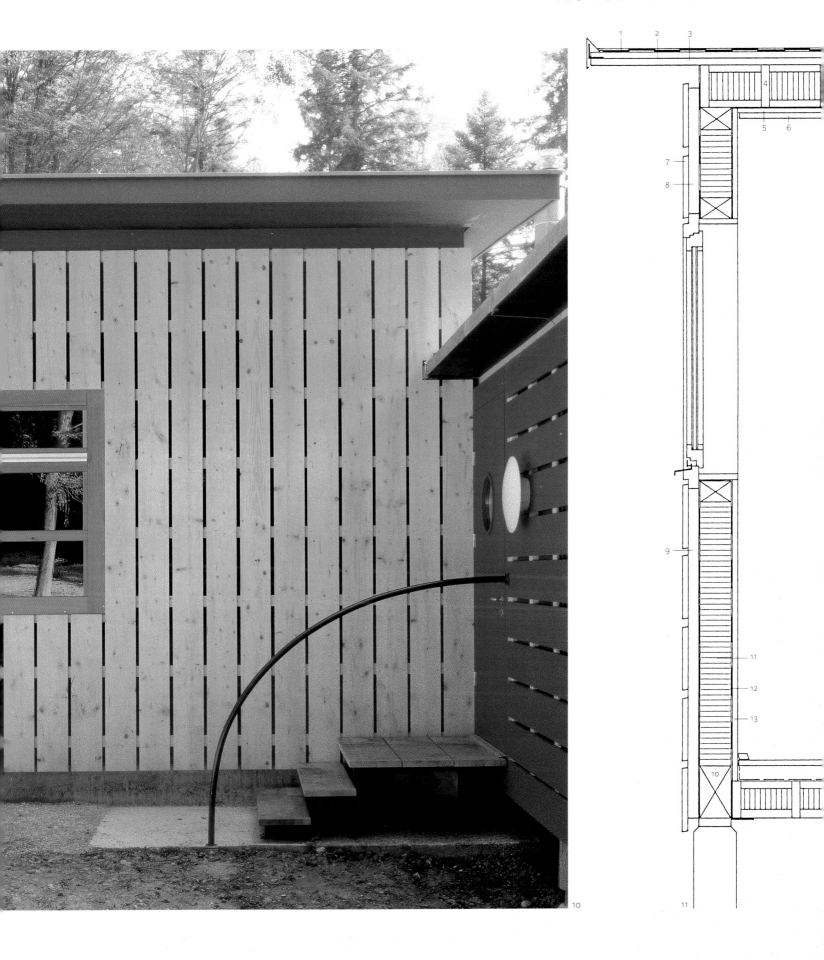

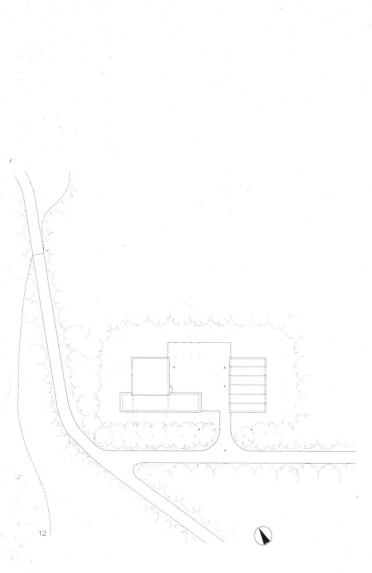

Rheinau forestry outpost
12. Site plan.
13. General view across the site.

14

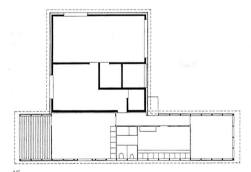

15

Rheinau forestry outpost
14. Entrance to the administration block.
15. Plan.
16. Shed, seen through trees.
17. Administration wing with garage behind.

16

Two forestry outposts
Client: Hochbauamt des Kantons
Zurich
Architect: Marianne Burkhalter
and Christian Sumi, Zurich,
Marianne Dutli, Andrea Bassi, Sybille
Bucher
Engineer: H. Hofacker and M. Krebs,
Zurich

17

1. Site plan.
2. Corner detail.

the administration room and conference area below. Despite the differences in construction technique, Baumschlager and Eberle have treated the building as a unified visual whole. Sandwich walls of larch (the local vernacular material) clad both levels and merge seamlessly with the roof so that, from the exterior, the building appears to be made entirely of timber. The overall design might be criticized as being somewhat contrived, or for drawing heavily for its inspiration on both the work of the British architect Peter Wilson (architect of the Münster library) and Juha Jääskeläinen, Juha Kaakko, Petri Rouhiainen, Matti Sanaksenaho and Jari Tirkkonen's Finnish Pavilion at Expo '92. Nevertheless, with its structure reminiscent of an upturned boat or wooden instrument, the Holz Altenried showroom and warehouse powerfully illustrates the expressive possibilities of wood construction.

This is architecture as billboard. Sitting beside a federal highway near Hergatz in Germany, Baumschlager & Eberle's sculptural wood form is an excellent advertisement for the timber company, Holz Altenried, which commissioned the building as a showroom and warehouse. As in advertising, however, all is not what it seems. Despite its external appearance, the two-storey building is part concrete and part timber in construction. Set into the slope of the land, the lower-ground floor is a heavy-duty storeroom. This is where trucks come in and load up with timber, which is stored here and in the timber yard behind. This lower part of the building, which takes quite a battering from heavy machinery, is made of concrete. Seven big loading bays, accessed from the rear of the building, plus a two-bay conference room, determine the organization of the space and the positioning of structural columns. In contrast, the upper floor, where the showroom is situated, is wood-framed, made up of ten laminated spruce portals of varying heights which rest on the concrete box below. Customers access the showroom via a ramp that leads from the highway up to a pair of glazed doors and into the space. The doors bring daylight into the brightly painted space, as do the twelve circular skylights and the long, low window that runs almost the entire length of the building. Three short slits incised into the southernmost corner light the small office and

7

Showroom and warehouse

Hergatz, Germany, 1994–95

Baumschlager & Eberle

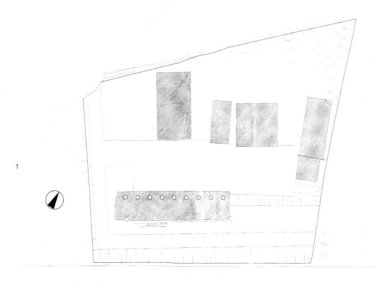

1

Showroom and warehouse
3. Laminated arches being craned into place.
4. Cross-section.
5. Rear elevation.
6. Front elevation.
7. Long section.

3

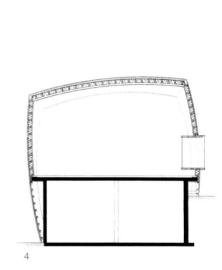

4

5

6

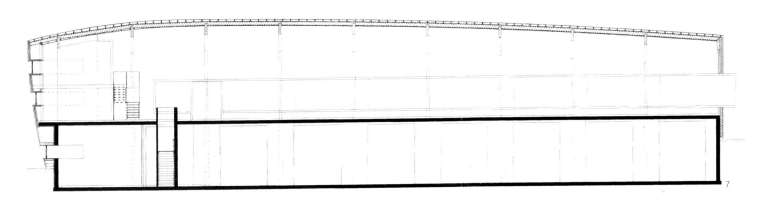

7

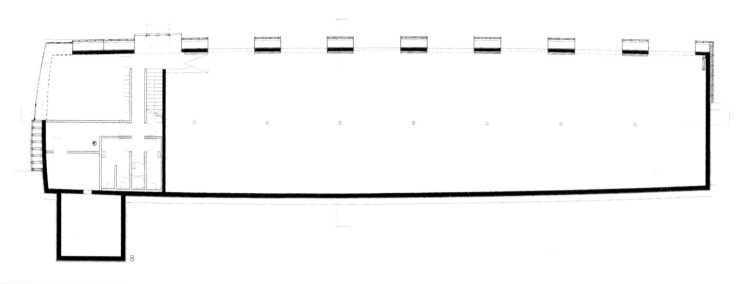

8

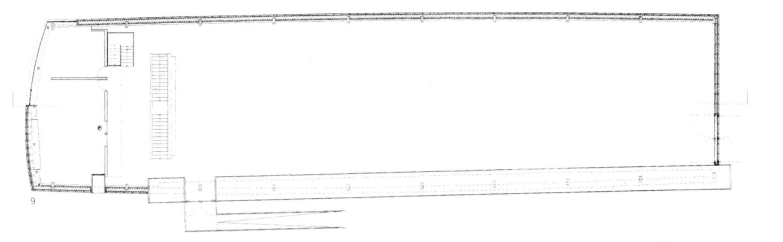

9

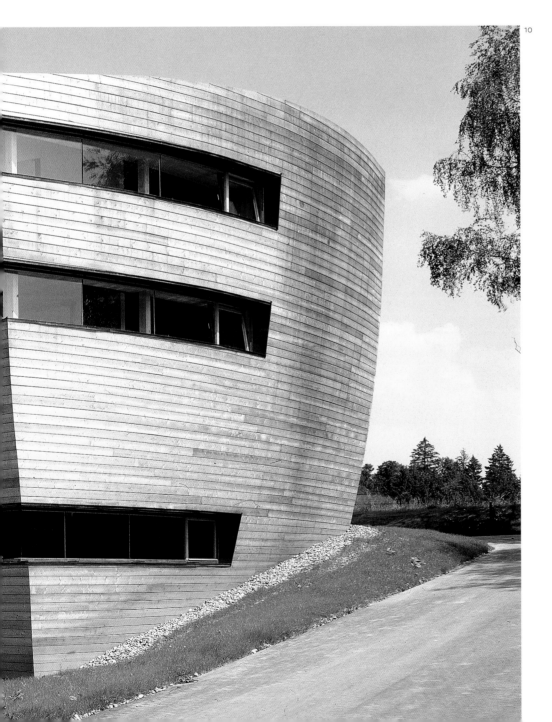

10

Showroom and warehouse
8. Ground-floor plan.
9. First-floor plan.
10. Rear and side elevations.

Showroom and warehouse
Architect: Baumschlager & Eberle
Planning: Architekturbüro B&E
Ges. m.b.H
Project manager: Oliver Baldauf
Assistance: Dipl. Ing. Michael
Ohneberg
Structural designer: Dipl. Ing. Plankel

Utilizing both new materials and the increased flexibility in engineering now attainable

through advanced computer-aided design programs, the buildings in this chapter have

been selected for the architects' sophisticated use of wood. Problematic structures,

including a toroidal dome, a massive volume and a large-span building constructed

from bamboo have been created thanks to a timely use of advanced technology.

STRUCTURAL POSSIBILITIES

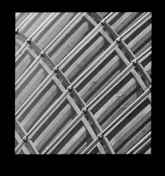

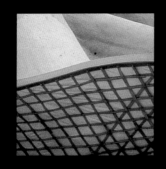
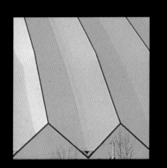

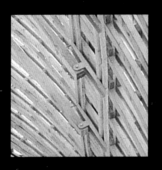
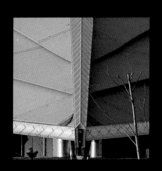
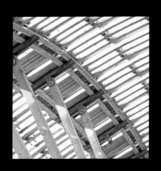

Enduring, easy to work and beautiful, wood has for thousands of years been one of mankind's primary building materials. But whether the wood is used in post-and-beam structures or log cabin-style constructions, the design of wooden buildings is limited by the length of a piece of timber, and by its uneven behaviour in tension and compression.

The development of glue-laminated timber (or glulam) has radically changed all this and has contributed in no small part to the current interest in wood as a building material. Glue-laminated timber is made from layers of accurately cut smaller timber sections, continuously glued together with an adhesive resin. It is a highly even material and can be made into beams up to 50 metres (160 feet) in length. A number of the buildings in this chapter, such as Niels Torp Architects' Olympic Hall in Hamar, Norway (see pages 84–89), with its huge 96-metre (315-foot) span (requiring two massive glue-laminated beams), would never have been possible without the use of these modern timbers.

Not all the buildings shown here rely on new types of materials, however. A number, like Samyn et Associés' Forestry centre in Belgium (see pages 76–83), are built from conventional timber, but employ construction methods that are only

1

1. Forestry centre, Samyn et Associés.
2. Naiju Community Centre, Shoei Yoh
+ Architects.
3. Olympic Hall, Niels Torp Architects.

2

possible thanks to advanced computer-aided design programs. High-powered computing is the second theme linking many of the buildings in this chapter.

Samyn et Associés' building is an incredibly intricate structure; a toroidal dome made up of a lattice of steam-bent timber elements that become progressively more complex as they rise to the building's apex. There is an argument, of course, that computers allow architects to design needlessly complicated buildings. There is some truth in this; the Forestry Centre is visually striking and structurally intriguing, but could perhaps be deemed over-engineered, a case of computing power getting the better of common sense.

In many other buildings, though, computers have helped create structures that, while ingenious, have an obvious rationale. This is certainly the case with the two Japanese examples in this chapter: Kajima Design's Izumo Dome (see pages 90–95) and Shoei Yoh's Naiju Community Centre (pages 96–101). In both of these examples, a simple idea is pushed to its logical conclusion. The Dome uses the ancient technology of the Japanese paper umbrella which, when scaled up through the use of computers, helps to create an enormous building that is unfurled on site with the aid of a hydraulic jack

and little else. The framework for the Naiju Community Centre, meanwhile, comprises a lattice of bamboo canes that is bent to form a delicate structure reminiscent of nothing so much as the peaks that napkins are folded into in smart restaurants.

The buildings discussed in this chapter are at the cutting edge of building design. Whether through advancements in the development of timber products, or the increasing use of computers to shape buildings, technological changes are helping to make timber an easier and more predictable material for architects to use.

3

1. Site plan.
2. Detail of the interior of the dome.

building where they meet the concrete substructure as a single element. Rising up, each arch becomes progressively wider, expanding to two, three and then four elements as it flattens out. The timber frame is impregnated with insecticide and fungicide, to prevent rot, and is clad on the outside in tiles of reflective tempered glass which are glued in place with silicone. Inside, the dome shelters two smaller concrete-block structures that run its full length. This both creates a clear central nave and provides secondary support for the arches. These structures house the cold storage, on one side, and offices, on the other. The nave is left clear for the large machines that treat and dry the seeds. The dome's wood and glass fabric provides little protection from the cold. In winter, radiant panels suspended off the inner structures are used to keep the seedlings – and the workers – warm. Curving ducts suspended from the roof can, when required, suck moist air from under the roof, to eliminate the condensation and excess humidity caused by plants. In summer, a series of vents along the bottom of the dome are employed to pull in fresh air. Stale air is drawn up through ducts and expelled over the west door. The building's reflected laminated glass envelope and complex timber structure act as a sunshade in summer, protecting the vulnerable specimens below as well as helping to keep staff comfortable. The shade cast by nearby trees provides additional protection.

High-tech engineering meets traditional materials and techniques in the forestry centre designed by Belgian architects and engineers Samyn et Associés. Set in the heart of Belgium's Ardennes Forest, the regional government-run centre provides facilities for testing, storing and cultivating seeds gathered from the area's historic woodlands. Its appropriately pod-shaped structure houses a large workshop together with a series of cold storage areas and a few offices and laboratories. Samyn et Associés' building is a toroidal dome (a portion of a doughnut-shaped, rather than spherical, surface), which allows for greater repetition of identical elements than would be possible with a sphere, making it cheaper to construct and to clad. The choice of form relates to an earlier proposal to use thinnings for the main structural elements, an idea which had to be abandoned after tests showed that thinnings cracked when dried rapidly. (Industrially dried steam-bent timber had to be used instead.) The building's form remains, however: a modern-day homage to the traditional use of bent timber and thinnings which can be found in buildings from Mongolian yurts to Zulu roundhouses. The structure comprises a series of complex, double-layered arches that branch into progressively more rectangular elements as they rise towards the building's highest point, from the rim of the concrete apron to which they are clamped. Stiffened by a spine running lengthways, the arches start at the base of the

8

Forestry centre

Marche-en-Famenne, Belgium

1992

Samyn et Associés

1

3

Forestry centre

3. The entrance to the forestry centre.
4. Ground-floor plan.
5. First-floor plan.
6. A toroid is a section of a doughnut-
shaped ring.
7. Long elevation.
8. Short elevation.
9. View of the dome in its setting.

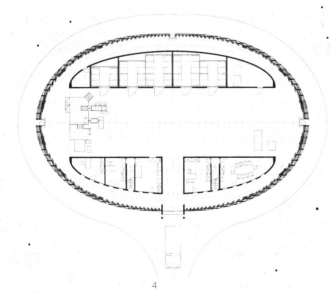

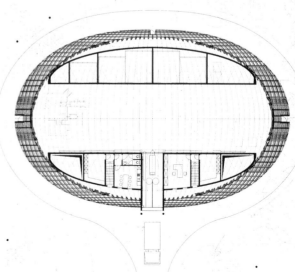

4

5

6

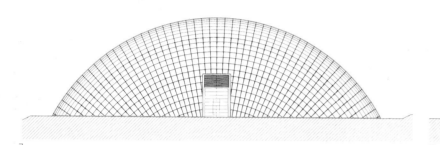

7

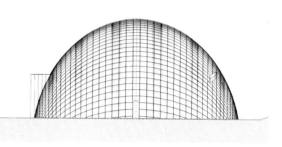

8

9

11

Forestry centre

10. View down the side of the building.

11. Close-up of the tempered glass panels which clad the building.

12. Part of the long section.

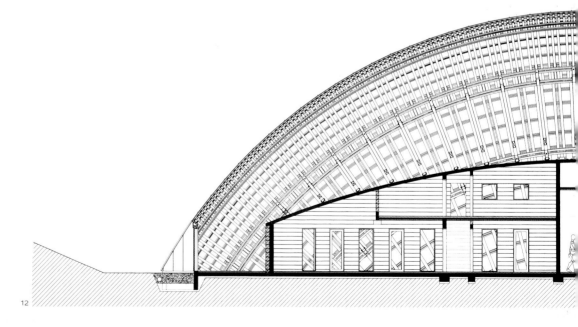

12

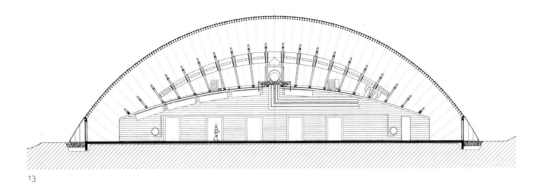

13

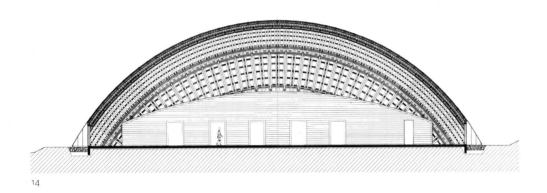

14

15

16

Forestry centre
Architect: Philippe Samyn (Samyn and Partners)
Project team: Ghislain André, Richard Delaunoit, Denis Mélotte, Bernard Vleurick
Structural engineer: Philippe Samyn, Guy Clautin (Samyn and Partners, Setesco)
Quantity surveyors: Samyn and Partners
Services engineers: Philippe Samyn, Paul Fontaine, André De Windt (Samyn and Partners, FTI)

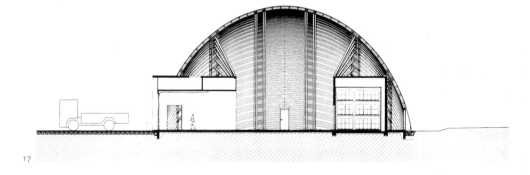

17

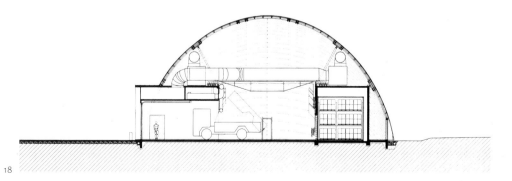

18

1. Site plan.
2. Interior view.

arched trusses, each chord of which is made from four pieces of laminated soft-wood bolted together. These trusses are supported on concrete props raised 1.5 metres (5 feet) above the main base structure. Ten different lengths of truss are used to fit the building's distinctive, elongated shape. The whole thing is stabilized by a huge longitudinal truss, that runs like a keel down the length of the roof. Inside, windows between the props bring daylight into the bottom of the building. Light also filters in through long thin slits in the steps of the roof decking. The main purpose of the slits, however, is to let light out, illuminating the building's distinctive shape at night and giving it a longitudinal emphasis – akin to the planks of a ship – that contrasts with the horizontal structural arches. So large a building (it rises to the height of an 11-storey building at its tallest point), with its huge structural elements, could easily look crude and chunky. Torp has alleviated this in the interior by focusing on the details, making sure that the laminated wooden arches and the joints where the windbraced steel construction meets the concrete frame of the arena were crisply finished. Some of the finer detailing proposed by Torp was sacrificed as being too expensive. The oiled iron doors and snowcatcher on the roof were jettisoned for instance, as was some of the signage. On the whole, however, the building is elegantly resolved; without doubt it put Hamar on the international map.

Several buildings vie for the title of the world's largest wooden structure, and Niels Torp Architects' Olympic Hall in Hamar is one of them. Built for the 1994 Winter Olympics, the indoor skating arena seats 13,000 spectators, covers 25,000 square metres (270,000 square feet) and used 2,000 cubic metres (70,600 cubic feet) of laminated timber. Beside the sheer technical difficulties of building so large a volume, the architects were faced with the problem of finding a design that would not overwhelm the small town. Hamar is a fishing town 50 kilometres (30 miles) south-east of the ski resort of Lillehammer where most of the Olympic events were held. Although it is near the mountains, the surrounding landscape around Hamar is flat. 'To design such a large building in the powerful flat Åkersvika [regional] landscape, exposed to everyone, is a task which puts one's self-confidence on trial,' comments Torp. The architect's solution was to focus on the form of the roof, the building's most visible element. By shaping this like the hull of an *oselver* – the beautiful type of wooden boat produced in Norway since the time of the Vikings – Torp gave the stadium a resonance with the ancient landscape. It looms in its surroundings like an upturned shipwreck, and possesses an iconic quality to which people could relate. Boat-building may be a Norwegian speciality but to design a hull on so large a scale required sophisticated computer modelling. The structure consists of a series of

9

Olympic Hall

Hamar, Norway, 1992

Niels Torp Architects

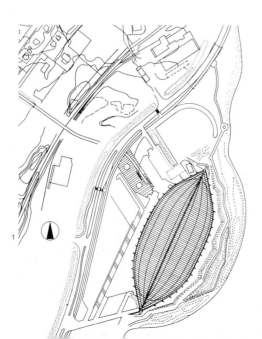

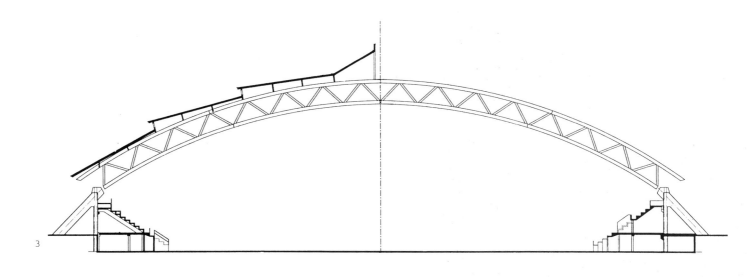

3

4

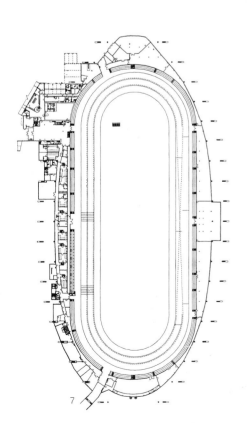

5

Olympic Hall
3. Cross-section showing roof structure.
4. Roof ridge.
5. Long interior view.
6. Detail of trusses.
7. First floor.
8. Second floor.
9. Third floor.

6

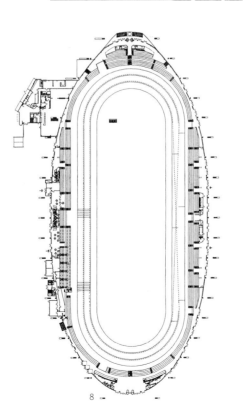

7

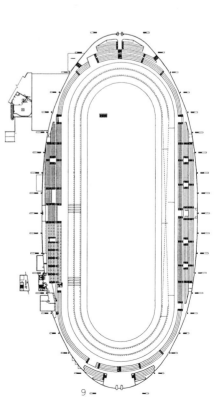

8

9

10

Olympic Hall

10. Detail of the concrete piers.
11. The finished building looming in the landscape. Its enormous bulk was reduced by painting the roof a deep blue−grey colour which blends in with the icy surroundings.
12. The roof sweeps down to meet the ground.
13. The Hall under construction.

11

12

Olympic Hall
Architect: Niels Torp AS; Biong & Biong
Arkitektkontor A/S
Project team: Niels A. Torp, Terje
Rørby, Kjell Beite, Paul Henrik Biong,
Jan Inge Lindeberg,
Structural engineer: Stormorken og
Hamre
Main contractor: Ole K. Karlsen AS

13

1. Site plan.
2. The erect dome.

ally checked. Once in place, the temporary ties were removed and steel props and tension ties put in place on the unclad pairs of beams. Finally, these were clad and the jacks removed. The process sounds complicated but in fact it is quite swift; it also requires very little high-level work, making it cheap and safe. Inside, the dome is light and airy. Daylight penetrates its Teflon-coated material skin so that artificial lighting is generally needed only after dark. The skin is also a good insulator, keeping the large unheated volume under the dome warm in winter. In summer, perimeter windows can be opened to create cross-ventilation that keeps the building cool. Most of the interior is taken up with a large sports pitch which is used for events ranging from sumo to American football. Spectators sit in one of two banks of seating: a fixed stand, located above the storage and machine rooms, or a movable stand at right angles to it. Otherwise the space is empty, allowing organizers to arrange it as they wish. The dome is being viewed by the architects as an experiment. Since it was constructed in 1992 numerous tests have been carried out to check its thermal performance and determine how the structure withstands different weather conditions. So far it has coped well with heavy snow loads, high winds and the extremes of hot and cold. Given its ease of erection and low cost, it is likely that we shall soon be seeing similar structures elsewhere.

The Izumo Dome is a deceptively simple-looking structure. Mimicking the mechanism of the Japanese umbrella or *janomegasa*, the 143 metre (470 foot) diameter building was erected in much the same way that an umbrella is pulled closed, with laminated timber and steel ties substituting for bamboo and string. The finished dome appears to be the product of straightforward building technology. In reality, however, it could never have been built without advanced computer modelling techniques. Designed by the Japanese engineering and architectural group Kajima, the dome houses a year-round, low-maintenance sports stadium. It was commissioned by the local authority of Izumo (a town in the central Japanese prefecture of Shimane) to celebrate the fiftieth anniversary of the town's founding. The structure uses American laminated timber drilled and bolted together on site to form 36 half-arches that are 90 metres (295 feet) long. Laid out to form a radial pattern, each arch was pin-jointed to a central steel ring at one end and, at the other, placed on a skid that was raised above the short concrete column on which it would eventually rest. Every other pair of arches was clad in a Teflon-coated fabric and secured together by steel props and tension ties. These were then held in place by temporary radial ties. Two 200-ton jacks then slowly raised the assembled structure in two phases (the first taking three days, the second five days), while the alignment was continu-

10

Izumo Dome

Izumo, Japan, 1992

Kajima Design

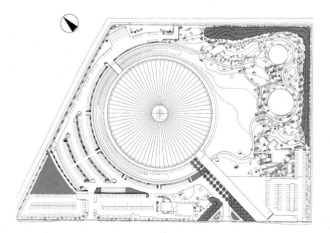

1

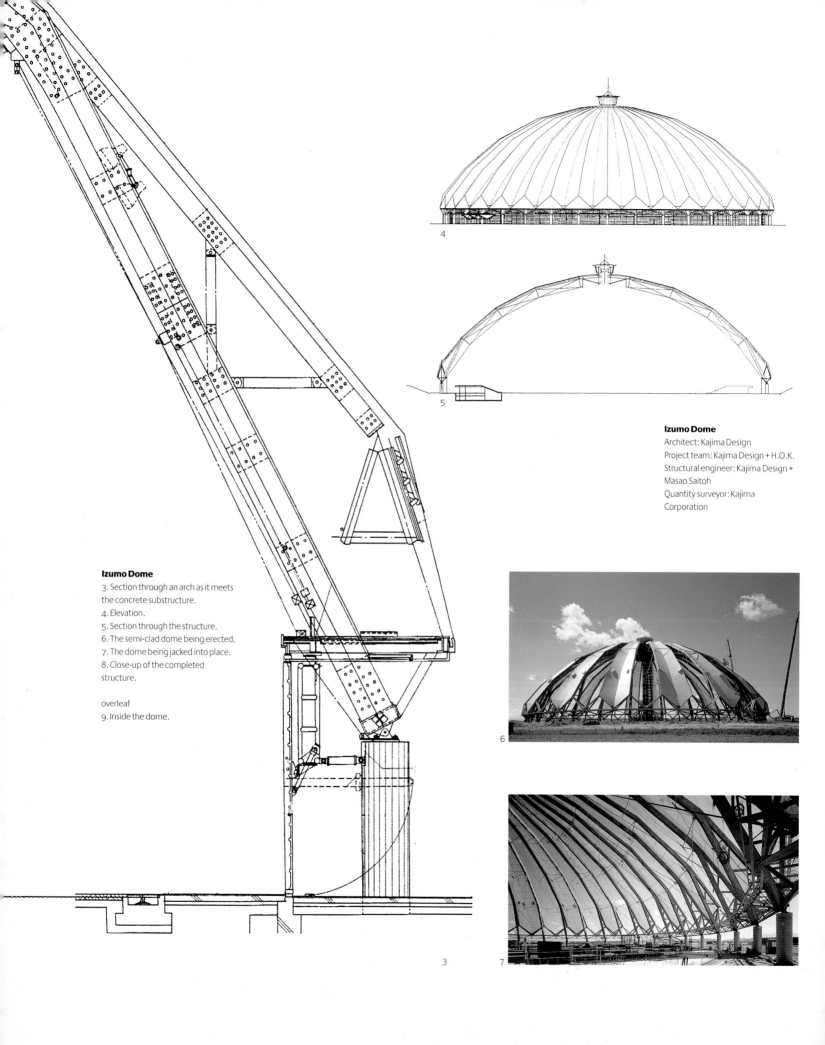

Izumo Dome

3. Section through an arch as it meets the concrete substructure.
4. Elevation.
5. Section through the structure.
6. The semi-clad dome being erected.
7. The dome being jacked into place.
8. Close-up of the completed structure.

overleaf
9. Inside the dome.

Izumo Dome

Architect: Kajima Design
Project team: Kajima Design + H.O.K.
Structural engineer: Kajima Design + Masao Saitoh
Quantity surveyor: Kajima Corporation

1. Diagram of the structure laid flat
and pulled into shape.
2. View inside the structure looking
up.

and nursery school. Because of the desire for a large element of local and community participation this is actually one of his simpler structures, despite its flower-like form. The structure began as a square grid, woven flat on the ground and like a giant piece of chair caning. Its centre was then raised on temporary posts (pegged to the ground at the edges), which were bent using heat and held in place for five weeks to produce an intricately folded structure. Finally, the posts were removed and the exterior of the structure covered in a layer of steel mesh and concrete to fix its striking folded form in place and give it strength. This, of course, means that the structure is in actual fact a concrete shell, but its complex shape would have been impossible without the bamboo groundwork which is the visually dominant element of the interior. The space covered by the great undulating roof is of the same area as the bamboo lattice-work before it was stretched and bent. This is divided into a large open-plan hall and a series of smaller auxiliary rooms. Both areas are deliberately straight-forward spaces, flexible enough to be used for a variety of local activities from nursery classes to small-scale musical recitals. Despite this pragmatism, the building is an extremely pleasant one, flooded with sunshine from the large glazed hole in the roof and light from perimeter windows that illuminate its dramatic bamboo lining.

Although Japan remains a heavily forested country, its forestry industry is in trouble. The country's slow-growing cedar forests are increasingly depleted, the result of the massive rebuilding programme after the Second World War, together with more recent social and economic changes, which have led land-owners to clear large tracts of forest. So when Shoei Yoh + Architects were commissioned to build a community centre and nursery school in the small southern Japanese town of Chikuho they looked to an alternative material: bamboo. Wood is the traditional building material in Japanese architecture – Kyoto and Nara have timber temples that are over a thousand years old – but nowadays the authorities no longer permit the construction of wood build-ings of more than 3,000 square metres (5,280 square feet) or over 15 metres (49 feet) in height. Yoh therefore had to obtain special permission to use bamboo in the community centre and nursery school. This bureaucracy was, he felt, worth it because of the significance that bamboo has to the local area. Plentiful and relatively cheap, indigenous bamboo is used in the Chikuho bamboo-shoot canning industry and so seemed an appropriate material for a local community project. Yoh is known for his large-span, geometrically com-plex buildings. Yet even his most intricate designs always clearly reveal how they were made. This is particularly true of the Naiju community centre

11

Naiju Community Centre

and Nursery School

Fukuoka, Japan, 1994

Shoei Yoh + Architects

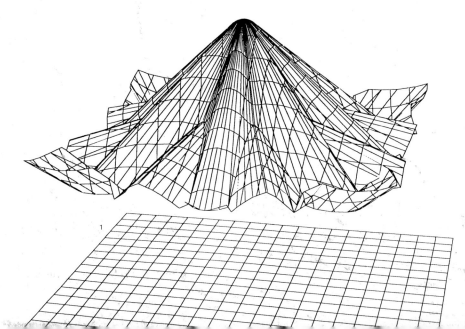

1

**Naiju Community Centre
and Nursery School**
3. The building under construction:
the bamboo grid is assembled flat.
4 + 5. Using poles as props, the
structure is gradually erected.
6. Inside, the centre of the structure is
supported by a temporary post.
7. The completed building.
8. Plan.

3

4

5

6

7

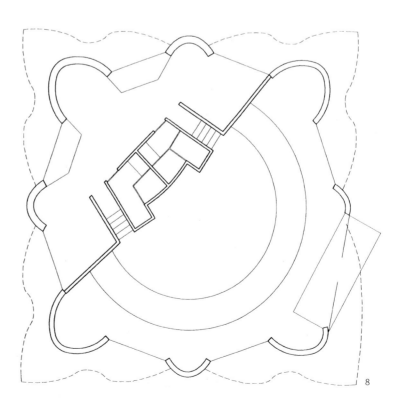

8

**Naiju Community Centre
and Nursery School**

9 + 10. Cross-sections.

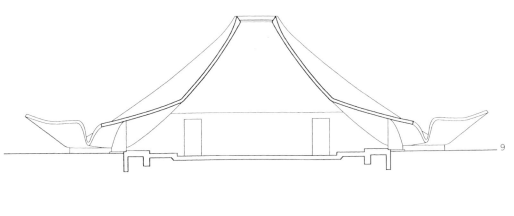

9

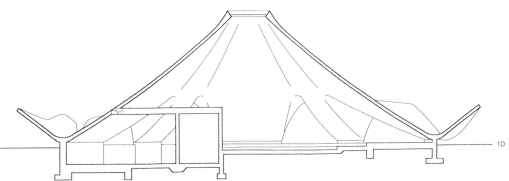

10

**Naiju Community Centre
and Nursery School**
11. Detail showing concrete cladding
over the bamboo substructure.
12. Peripheral windows help light the
building.

11

**Naiju Community Centre and
Nursery School**
Architects: Shoei Yoh + Architects
Structural engineering: Kusaba
Structural Design + Gengo Matsui +
Yoichi Minagawa
Mechanical and electrical
engineering: Ariyoshi Mechanical
Engineers + Fujino Electrical Engineers

The use of wood in sustainable architecture comes in various forms. The following archi-

tects have all built with sustainably sourced timber, for a wide range of uses and sizes,

including several buildings that make use of low-grade, and thus normally discarded,

timber. Structures that employ solar power and natural ventilation are highlighted; the

raison d'être here is buildings that actively benefit the planet, that are therefore 'green'.

GREEN BUILDINGS

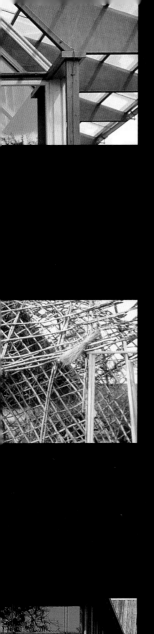

1

The hole in the ozone layer grows larger every day; climate changes are accelerating, with reports of freak weather conditions – hurricanes, droughts and floods – becoming ever more frequent; distressing images of the destruction caused to lives and property fill our TV screens on a regular basis. While environmental pressure groups lobby governments to cut so-called 'greenhouse gases', a growing number of scientists believe a different solution is called for. British scientist James Lovelock, among others, claims that man-made increases in emissions of carbon dioxide – the major 'greenhouse gas' – are relatively insignificant compared with the massive amounts of carbon dioxide naturally produced by the planet. What is going wrong, he and others argue, is that the earth's mechanism for dealing with carbon dioxide is being thwarted. The remedy is more trees.

Trees are essential to the safe and balanced working of the biosphere. They regulate our climate and stabilize the water content in the soil and air, as well as providing food and shelter for animals and humans alike. Like all plants, they also extract carbon dioxide from the atmosphere, transforming it into life-sustaining oxygen. So not only is wood the only building material that can be regrown, but also – as long as it is grown in a sustainable way in managed plantations where a new tree is planted for every mature felled one – it is actively beneficial to the planet.

1. Centre for Understanding the
Environment, Horniman Museum,
Architype.
2. Two-family house, Herzog +
Partner.
3. Olivier Theatre, Oak Design Group.

2

Environmental concerns are one of the key reasons for the current popularity of wood as a building material. Throughout its life cycle wood is one of the most environmentally friendly of building materials. Timber's 'embodied energy' – the energy required in its production – is less than that of aluminium, brick, concrete, plastics or steel. In requiring more energy to make, these materials all lead to increased carbon dioxide emissions. Furthermore, timber can easily be recycled; when disposed of through rotting or burning, it is returned to nature without any further energy input.

All the buildings shown in this chapter are built from sustainably sourced timber. A number also tackle the problem of what to do with timber that is not good enough to sell as lumber. Some of this can of course be pulped and made into wood byproducts such as particle board and fibreboard (such as MDF), but there is still tremendous waste in the system. In trying to find a use for timber that is normally discarded, David Lea's painter's studio (pages 126–131) and Edward Cullinan Architects' Westminster Lodge (pages 132–137) both explore ways of using 'thinnings' – outcuts which are insufficiently straight or strong to be sold as lengths of timber and which are usually simply burnt as waste– as a structural material.

A number of the examples harness natural forces. This might be by using the building's orientation to ensure that the sun heats it (in the case of Thomas Herzog's house, on pages 106–113); employing solar power to water a grass roof (Architype's extension to the Horniman Museum, pages 120–125); or using natural ventilation (as in the theatre designed by Feilden Clegg Architects, pages 114–119). But the major force in shaping buildings will always be humankind. Architype's self-build housing estate (pages 138–143) is included in this chapter on 'green' buildings not so much because the materials and system used are environmentally friendly (although they are), but because the process of self-building teaches people about buildings and their environmental impact. Through knowledge comes the power to demand better, more responsible buildings.

3

1. Short section through the house.
2. End elevation.

thick. Sailing over the whole structure is the dramatic roof; this is covered in cor-rugated sheet metal above the building's central zone, but extends in glass over the corridors and beyond the building's envelope. It is planned to cover the glass with photo-voltaic cells at a later stage. Glass is also the primary material on much of the building's south elevation. Naturally, this creates problems of heat loss and gain. Some solar protection is provided by the first-floor balcony which, cantilevered off the south elevation, helps shade the lower rooms. In summer, some shade is provided by the climbing plants which grow up trellises on the south side of the building. In addition, the building benefits from a ventilation heat-recovery plant, which uses heat from the outgoing air to warm the fresh incoming air. As well as these now relatively well-accepted thermal measures, Herzog has experimented with a more unusual technique. Integrated into four of the ground-floor bays on the building's south façade is a translucent thermal insulation panel 10cm (4 inches) thick, which soaks up heat during the day and radiates it internally during the evening and night. The house was the first build-ing to use this 'warm wall' technique which was developed by the Freiburg Insti-tute for Solar Energy Systems. Herzog's combination of methods appears to work well; additional radiators are only needed on the coldest of winter days and the client has a home that is filled for most of the year with sunshine and light.

Thomas Herzog is well known in Germany for his environmental designs. Whilst his pioneering energy-efficient factory for furniture maker Wilkhahn received widespread recognition in the early 1990s, the equally forward-looking house that he designed in the Upper Bavarian town of Pullach is less well known. The client came to Herzog wanting a two-family home made from environmentally friendly materials and requiring little energy to run. Herzog's response has been to create a lightweight timber and glass structure which uses natural systems – energy-efficient materials, orientation, sunlight, planting, passive cooling – to maximum effect. Situated in the corner of a field, the two-storey house is long and narrow. The main living spaces form a central block which runs the length of each floor and is entered from corridors on either side. The layered spatial arrangement creates a degree of ambiguity between inside and out, an effect that is further reinforced by a balcony running along the building's south side at first-floor height. Despite the building's symmetrical section, its focus is this long, south-facing façade which opens up towards the field. The north eleva-tion, by contrast, abuts a bank of tall conifers. The house is constructed from a laminated timber frame with posts and cross-beams at 3.6 metre (12 foot) cen-tres. The frame is braced by a system of diagonal steel ties and clad (where not triple-glazed) in insulated panels of cement-bound chipboard 15cm (6 inches)

12

Two-family house

Pullach, Germany, 1990

Herzog + Partner

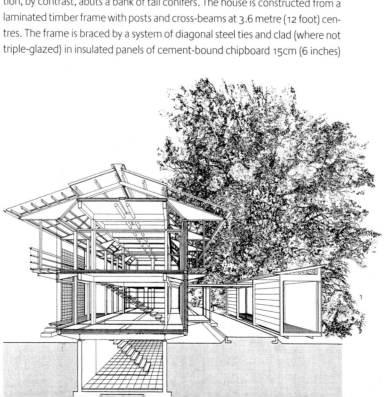

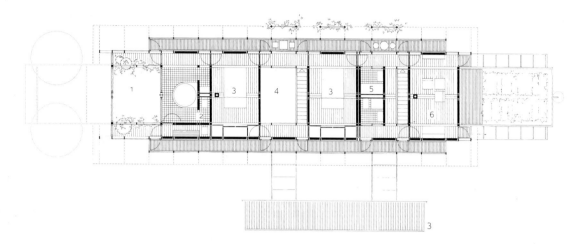

3

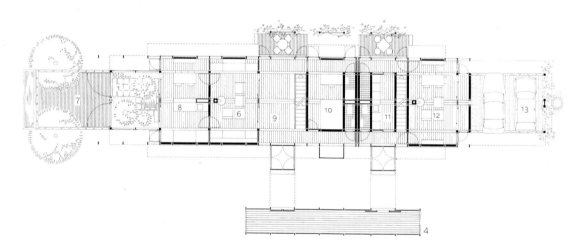

4

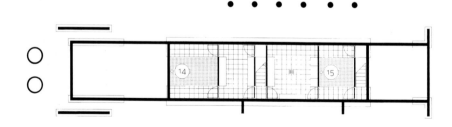

5

6

key

1 indoor garden
2 sauna/bathroom
3 bedroom
4 open area
5 bathroom/shower
6 living room
7 terrace
8 kitchen/dining room
9 hall
10 guest room
11 kitchen
12 dining room
13 carport
14 cellar 1
15 cellar 2

Two-family house

3. First-floor plan.
4. Ground-floor plan.
5. Basement-level plan.
6. South elevation.
7. End elevation with carport.

7

Two-family house
8. Construction detail through the external wall at ground-floor level.
9. Construction detail showing a cross-section through the building.
10. South-facing first-floor balcony.

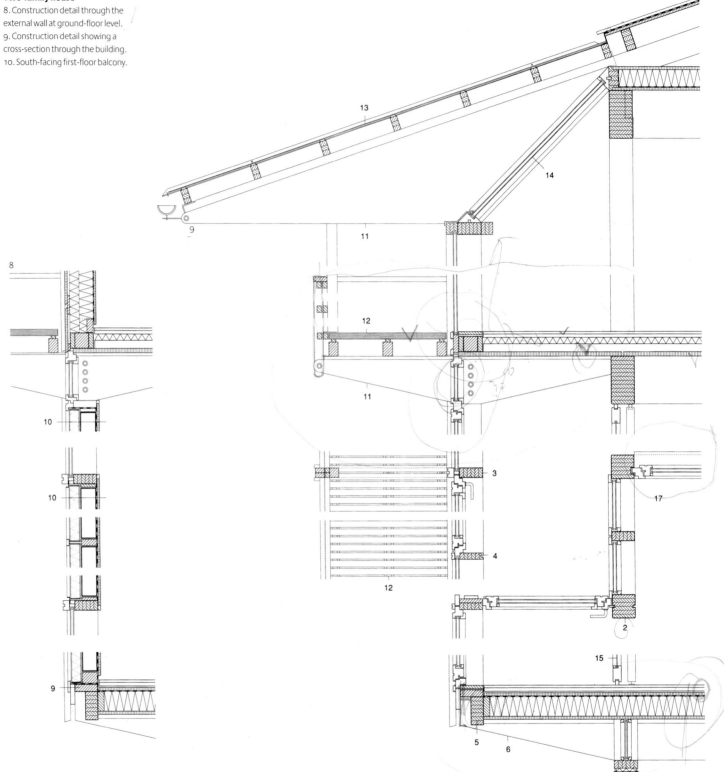

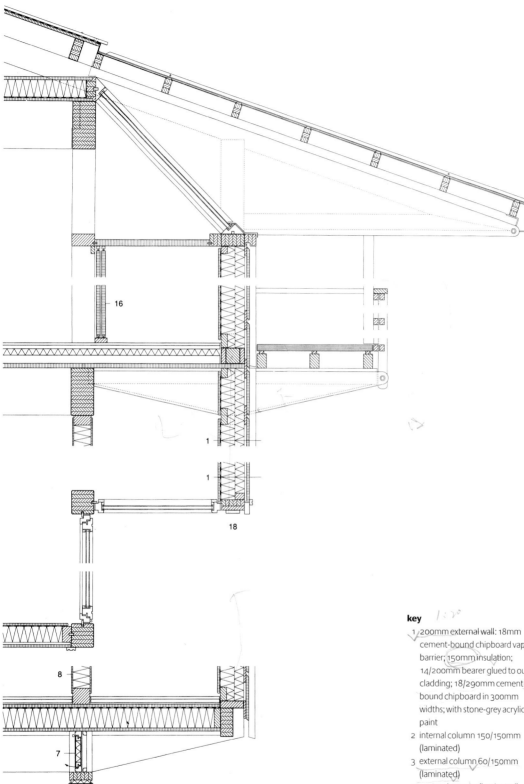

10

key

1 200mm external wall: 18mm cement-bound chipboard vapour barrier; 150mm insulation; 14/200mm bearer glued to outer cladding; 18/290mm cement-bound chipboard in 300mm widths; with stone-grey acrylic paint

2 internal column 150/150mm (laminated)

3 external column 60/150mm (laminated)

4 post 40/150mm (laminated)

5 edge beam 60/180mm (laminated)

6 beam 100/400mm (laminated)

7 ventilation flap with insect screen

8 internal wall

9 timber plate 50/150mm

10 heat-storage wall: 18mm cement-bound chipboard vapour barrier (polyethylene foil); 100mm precast-concrete element painted black externally; translucent thermal insulating element – capillary polycarbonate (matt) with horizontal linear structure, covered with glass

11 composite cantilevered member

12 timber strips 40/40mm

13 toughened-glass roof

14 double glazing with laminated inner sheet

15 glazed sliding doors

16 sliding doors to built-in cupboards

17 south-west corner of conservatory

18 north-east corner of building

12

Two-family house
Architect: Thomas Herzog
Partners: Michael Volz with
Michael Streib

Two-family house
11. Close-up of the laminated timber-frame structure and diagonal steel bracing.
12. View down the first-floor corridor.
13. A first-floor living room.

13

1. Short section through the foyer.
2. The barn-like structure of the foyer.

in quality). It is also less wasteful than dried oak, which has to be discarded if it warps and twists while drying. Oak Design Group's building consists of three parts: a double-height auditorium, a smaller foyer and backstage facilities. Each of these uses a different method of timber-frame construction, and is naturally ventilated. The structural frame of the 300-seat auditorium is made from four free-standing solid green oak corner posts, 8 metres (26 feet) high and 40 x 40cm (15 ¾ x 15 ¾ inches) in cross-section. These are joined at their heads by four trusses which, in turn, are met by four hips that continue up to a rooftop lantern. Rods hanging from the trusses support the balconies. The foyer area is a traditional, barn-like two-storey structure whose timber-frame construction contrasts with the more industrial methods used for the backstage area. Here, posts of Douglas fir, with softwood trusses at 8.1 metre (26 ½ foot) centres and strengthened by steel diagonal braces, create a box-like space that is used as a backstage workshop. All three parts of the building have untreated larch cladding on the exterior and home-grown softwood boarding inside. The trouble with using green oak of course, is that it warps and shrinks (by as much as 10 per cent across its section) as it dries. To deal with this, flexible seals, lapped joints in the flashings and adjustable wedges were incorporated into the structure, enabling it to be 'tuned' as it dries out over the first year of use.

Bedales stands at the maverick edge of the English public school tradition. Founded in the late nineteenth-century in the spirit of the Arts and Crafts movement, middle-class liberals have been sending their children here for generations, attracted by its mix of academic results and more artistic pursuits. Principal among these extra-mural activities is theatre. In 1993 the school commissioned Carpenter Oak & Woodland, a company specializing in oak frames, to design a new theatre. They, in turn, suggested bringing Feilden Clegg Architects, specialists in environmental design, on to the team. Working together, they called themselves Oak Design Group. The team's design approach was to continue the pioneering spirit behind the school's inception. In an early design document it argued: 'The new building is intended to provide a strong statement about the environmental view that should be embodied in architecture, both from the perspective of avoiding energy consumption and air conditioning, and in the utilization of materials which have an environmental impact.' The Olivier Theatre is one of the largest oak-framed structures in the UK. One of the reasons for choosing green (unseasoned) oak was that the school already has a number of important green oak-framed buildings, including an Arts and Crafts-style library. Another consideration was cost. While kiln-dried oak is expensive, green oak is relatively cheap (it costs little more than Douglas fir and is superior

13

Olivier Theatre

Bedales School, Petersfield,

Hampshire, UK, 1996

Oak Design Group

(Feilden Clegg Architects

and Roderick James)

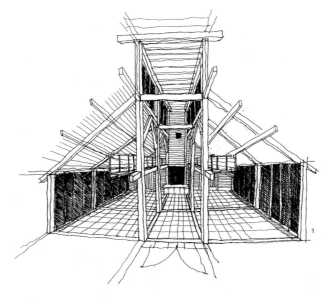

1

BEDALES OLIVIER THEATRE

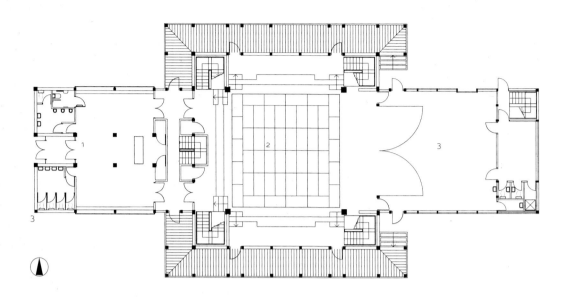

key
1 foyer
2 auditorium
3 backstage

3

4

Olivier Theatre

3. Ground-floor plan.

4. Short elevation showing the main entrance and foyer in the foreground with the larger volume of the auditorium behind.

5. View of the auditorium showing the green oak corner posts and roof trusses.

6. Section through the auditorium.

7. Long section.

5

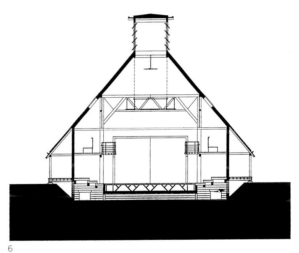

6

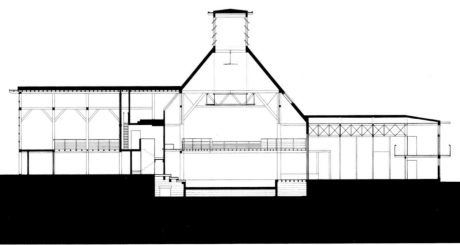

7

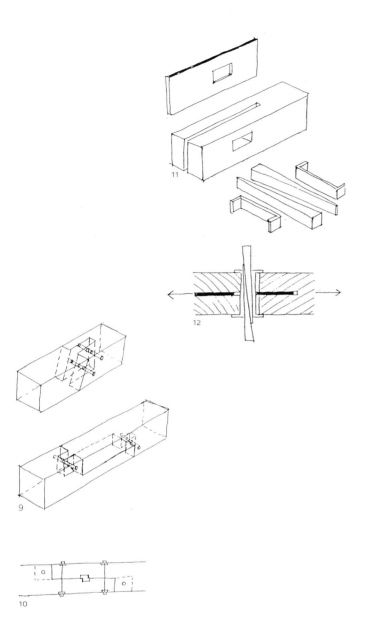

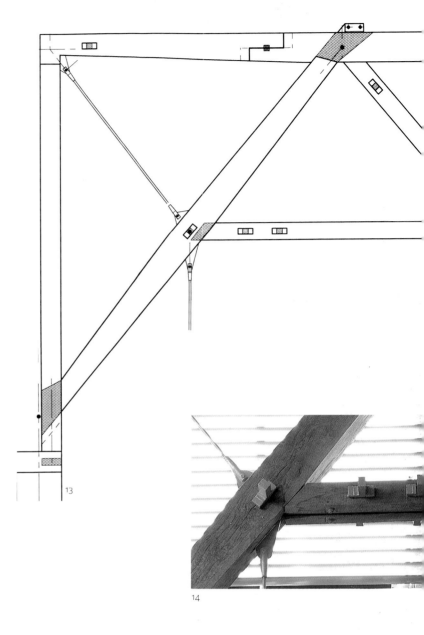

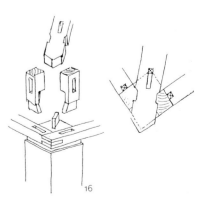

Olivier Theatre

8. Balcony-level in the auditorium.
9–12. Various jointing systems are used, including scarf joints (11), gib and cotter (12), tabled scarf joints (9) and keyed tabled scarf joints (10).
13 + 14. Gib and cotter joints in the main auditorium truss help reinforce the truss joints and make connections to the steel rods.
15. Dovetail tenon.
16. Head of post.

Olivier Theatre

Architects: Feilden Clegg Architects
Peter Clegg, Martin Benson, Anne Claxton
Roderick James Architects
Roderick James
Structural engineers: Duncan &Millais
Services engineers: Max Fordham & Partners
Project manager: Tim Battle and Rybka Battle, acting for Bedales School
Specialist oak frame consultants: Carpenter Oak & Woodland
Main contractor: Bedales School under the direction of Paul Buxey, Estates Manager

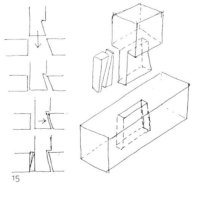

1. Site plan. The building is orientated northwards, facing towards the gardens, and away from a main arterial route out of London.
2. West elevation.

is the only triple-glazed space on the south side of the building. A reed bed situated under the building collects rainwater and recycles waste water (other than sewage). When the weather is good, photo-voltaic cells on the roof generate electricity, driving a pump that draws water up to the roof. This keeps the grass green and provides evaporative cooling for the building. This is a robust building with no attempt at slick or delicate detailing. The prefabricated structure is made from six hollow plywood columns with six triangular 21 metre (68 foot) long beams – three under the floor and three at ceiling height – threaded over them. The columns, ending as chimneys which are capped with aluminium hoods, pull air up from underneath the building. Air is diffused through slatted vents in the floor and the column bases. These ventilate the building in summer; in winter the ventilation holes underneath the building are sealed. Underfloor heating insulation help keep the spaces warm. The architects tried to minimize the energy needed to produce the building, and the levels of pollution it generates. For this reason they chose timber as the main building material, despite its low thermal mass. The plywood was imported from Scandinavia and Canada but the Welsh-grown Douglas fir cladding and interior plywood are local. All the finishes are non-polluting – the wood stains are organic, the floor is covered in environment-friendly linoleum and the chipboard is urea-free.

When, in 1896, Harrison Townsend designed an ethnographic museum in south London for the Victorian philanthropist Frederick Horniman, he created one of the finest British art nouveau buildings. One hundred years later the museum was extended with the addition of the Centre for Understanding the Environment, a building intended to be every bit as avant-garde as Townsend's original design. The idea behind the centre was to create a 'living exhibit', a place where schoolchildren could learn about natural and built environments through exhibitions, lectures and, just as importantly, through the building itself. Architype, the centre's architects, are seriously committed to ecological design, taking a holistic approach that considers the resource, energy and health implications of all aspects of their buildings. The Centre is typical of their work: it is built of wood, is naturally ventilated, and generates some of its own energy; wherever possible, non-polluting materials were used in its construction, and there is a reed bed to recycle waste water. The single-storey building has an awkward site in a corner of the museum's gardens. The building is organized in two halves, with the main exhibition space on the north side, and the audio-visual auditorium and seminar room on the south. A high-level clerestory brings sunshine into the exhibition space, which has triple-glazed windows running along its long elevation and a deck and ramp leading into the gardens. The seminar room

14

Centre for Understanding

the Environment,

Horniman Museum

London, UK, 1997

Architype

3

**Centre for Understanding the
Environment**
3. East elevation with link to the main
museum building.
4. Plan.
5. View of the west elevation from the
adjacent park.

key

1 music room
2 craft room
3 demonstration room
4 garden
5 bridge
6 access bridge
7 stream/reed bed/pond
8 exhibition
9 audio-visual auditorium
10 control
11 seminar room
12 wc
13 office

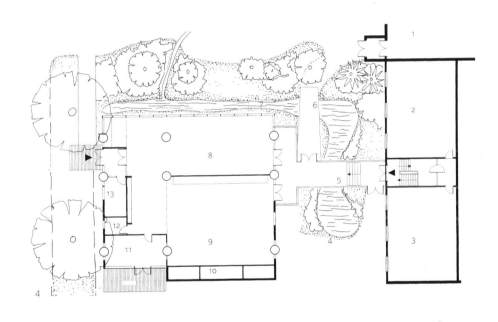

Centre for Understanding the Environment, Horniman Museum

Architect: Architype
Jonathan Hines, Tim Crosskey, Martin Hughes
Structural engineer: Stuart Richardson
Environmental engineer: Michael Popper Associates
Timber structure: Case Construction

Centre for Understanding the Environment

6. View showing how the structure is composed. Structural columns are threaded through hollow triangular beams and capped off with aluminium hoods.

7. The building is designed to minimize energy use. Using the chimneys to create a stack effect, fresh air is drawn from underneath the building into the main spaces. In winter, underfloor heating warms the air, which is then expelled through vents just below the ceiling.

8. In summer, cool air is again drawn into the building from below, via additional shafts in the column bases. The cool air circulates before being expelled. Additional, evaporative cooling is provided by watering the turf roof.

9. Detail of the roof, wall and floor structure.

10. View of the main exhibition space looking north-west.

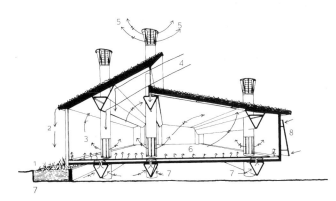

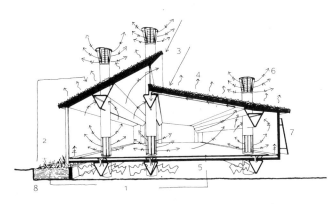

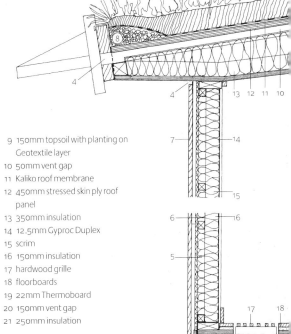

key

1. 450mm stressed skin ply floor panel
2. chamfered edge to form drip
3. 12mm ply
4. insect screen
5. 100 x 50mm vertical studs
6. 50 x 50mm horizontal battens at 600mm
7. ex 125 x 25mm boards on ex 75 x 25mm battens on 15mm bitumen softboard
8. 75mm land drain surrounded by shingle
9. 150mm topsoil with planting on Geotextile layer
10. 50mm vent gap
11. Kaliko roof membrane
12. 450mm stressed skin ply roof panel
13. 350mm insulation
14. 12.5mm Gyproc Duplex
15. scrim
16. 150mm insulation
17. hardwood grille
18. floorboards
19. 22mm Thermoboard
20. 150mm vent gap
21. 250mm insulation

10

Painter's studio
1. Drawing of the south elevation.
2. View along the south façade with the bay window which illuminates the principle seating area. The studio's bent wood bulges organically when covered with render.

dle of the building, dipping down to 3 metres/9 feet 10 inches), which creates the building's pointed ends, and by the curved gravel boards around the base, which tie the whole structure together. The main timbers were screwed into the gravel boards so that should the timber rot away, the structure will still be held together. The walls were then built up on a diagonal lattice made from thatch battens and a web of smaller timbers. This was filled with straw, covered in chicken wire and finally rendered inside and out. Equally inexpensive – and environmentally friendly – solutions were used to create the floor and roof. The floor consists of a 50mm (2 inch) layer of sand-and-cement screed, laid on top of a bed of stones and gravel that has simply been put straight on to the cleared topsoil. This is drained at the sides and built up with hard-core at the lower end. The roof is thatch, which is rendered inside. Morning and evening sun is ensured by the low bay window tucked in just below the roof line on one side of the building, and the glazed doors and windows at either end. This is a very small building without any of the mod cons that we all expect. While there is heating (in the form of a wood-burning stove) and running water, the studio has no electricity or toilet. The studio is obviously not a template for mass development, but at a cost of only £3,300 (in 1988), it is an example of a highly economic and environmentally sustainable alternative to brick and mortar that individuals can create for themselves.

Considering that one of its national symbols is the oak tree, Britain has treated its historic forests with little respect. Happily this is now changing, but these newly planted trees will take up to 150 years to mature. In the meantime, a vast percentage of timber used in the UK is imported. In the face of this, a handful of British architects have begun experimenting with thinnings – the small saplings taken out when coppicing or timber is not good enough for use as lumber – which are normally simply burnt as waste. Deep in a Somerset valley, the architect David Lea has designed a cottage using this very material. The 28 square-metre (300 square-foot) single-storey building houses a studio and sleeping platform for a painter and art teacher. The tiny cottage provides her with a space in which to work on the family-owned estate, away from the distractions of relatives. Despite its somewhat twee appearance, the building is a direct expression of its wooden structure; its concept is far from nostalgic. The building – which uses local materials that are both renewable and non-polluting – was built by the client to Lea's design, without employing heavy machinery or complicated woodworking. The first step was to embed a series of saplings (of 50mm/2 inches in base diameter) into the ground at 900mm (3 foot) intervals. Their tops were then bent over and lashed together to create an arch. Longitudinal stability was given both by varying the height of the saplings (which are 3.15 metres/10 feet 4 inches in the mid-

15

Painter's studio

Somerset, UK, 1988

David Lea

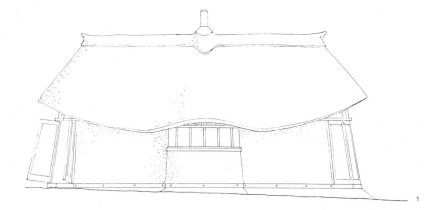

1

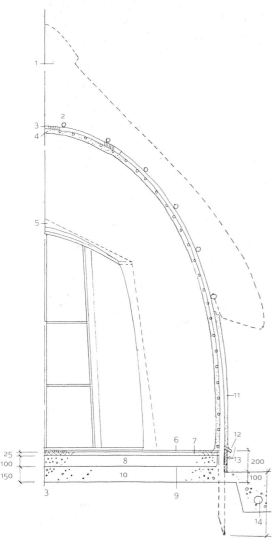

key

1. thatch
2. thatch battens
3. main loops
4. render
5. door/window frames
6. carpet
7. expanded polystyrene
8. gravel
9. 1000g polythene
10. gravel
11. render
12. fillet
13. gravel board
14. land drain

5

4

Painter's studio

3. Slice through the studio showing construction techniques.
4. The studio under construction.
5. The finished building nestles comfortably in the rolling Somerset countryside.
6. Section.

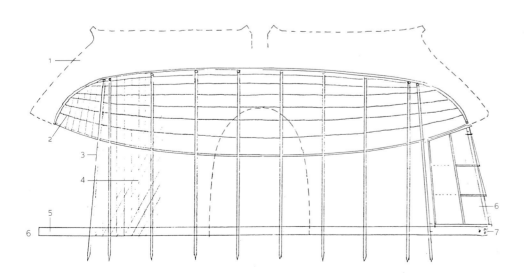

key

1 thatch
2 thatch battens
3 main hoops
4 lattice
5 gravel board
6 window/door frames
7 coach bolts

Painter's studio

7. Despite its small windows and low, sloping ceiling, the interior of the studio is light and airy.

8. Short section.

9. Detail of the interior. The studio has only rudimentary plumbing and heating.

10. Plan.

7

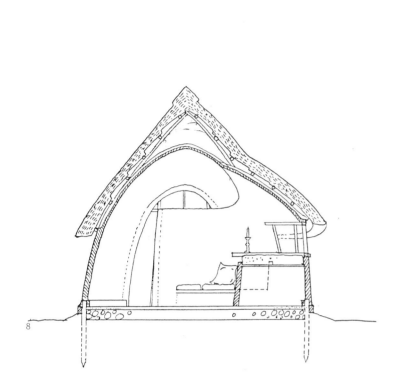

8

9

Painter's studio
Architect: David Lea
Project team: Client, family and
friends.

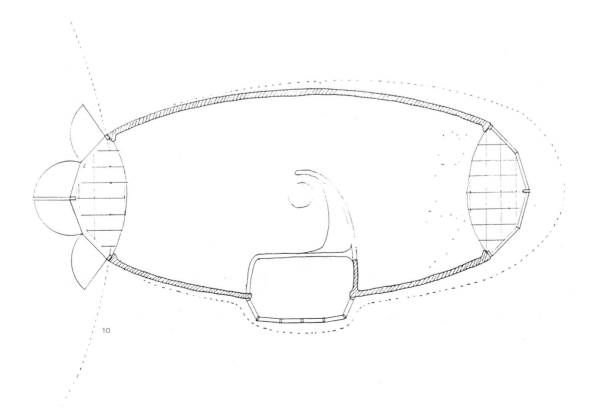

10

1. Site plan.
2. Detail showing the student accommodation slung between the overhanging roof and the posts that raise the building off the ground.

roundwood thinnings (so-called because thinnings are round in section, rather than square or rectangular like slats). Raised on posts above the forest floor, the building comprises four pairs of bedrooms, laid out in a cruciform plan, and a central communal space. The internal framed walls are made from roundwood and are soundproof. Thinnings are also used to support the glass roof over the central area. There they are bent over dividing walls and engineered into a double lattice; elsewhere the roof is turfed. The building is quirky; not every student will relish the lodge's spaceship-style form and unkempt aesthetic. But the accommodation is generous: each student has a 3x6 metre (10x20 foot) bedroom which includes a glass-reinforced-plastic pod of 1 metre (3 feet) diameter, containing a toilet and shower. The communal area has a small kitchen and a wood-burning stove. The building is seen as an experiment in timber technology. Designed by Edward Cullinan Architects, in close association with engineers Buro Happold and scientists at the University of Bath, it was part-funded by the Department of the Environment as part of a study it is doing into roundwood technology. At present the DoE does not officially recognize the use of roundwood in the UK Building Regulations. Having convincingly proved that a roundwood structure not only stands up but is also an environmentally-friendly alternative to timber or steel, the building's designers hope that roundwood will soon be permitted in the building codes.

Hooke Park is the scene of some of the most radical experiments in environmental architecture in Britain. The park is run by the Parnham Foundation, an organization that promotes wood craftsmanship both through its school, Parnham House, where young craftspeople are trained, and through its sponsorship of wood-related activities. Westminster Lodge was commissioned by the school's proprietor, furniture designer John Makepeace, who wanted an eight-bedroom block of student accommodation that would exemplify his beliefs in wood craftsmanship and environmental design. The building is the first of five that together will create an 'ecological village' at Hooke Park. Besides the accommodation block, the village will comprise a domed 'village hall' or community centre, an energy self-sufficient house, and two prototype houses, one for the countryside and one for urban areas. The buildings are all planned to exploit the structural properties of wood in new and innovative ways. One of Makepeace's interests is to promote the use of thinnings – young trees not straight or strong enough to be used as timber beams or joists. 'Britain imports 90 per cent of its timber, at an annual cost of £9 billion,' he declares. 'Yet thinnings, which represent half the annual crop of British timber, are disregarded as a structural material. By using this resource, we can improve the quality and productivity of UK woodlands, and reduce imports.' To this end, Westminster Lodge is built from locally resourced

16

Westminster Lodge

Hooke Park, Dorset, UK, 1996

Edward Cullinan

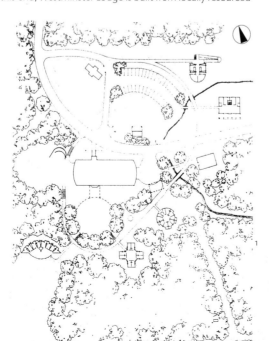

Westminster Lodge
3. The building has views out over the forest in all directions.

Westminster Lodge
4. View from the approach.
5. The building is decidedly quirky: some have accused it of resembling a space-ship landed in the college grounds.

4

5

6

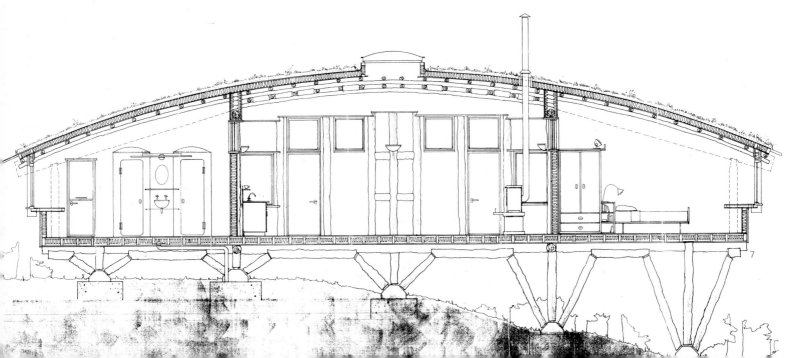

7

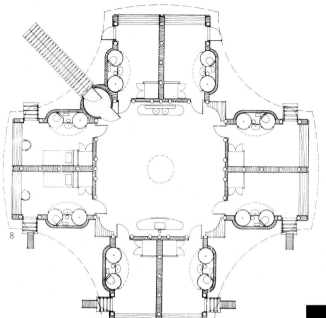

8

Westminster Lodge
Architects: Edward Cullinan,
John Romer, Sasha Bhavan
Project Manager: Don Stubbington
Foreman: John Bunford
Engineers: Buro Happold with
Bath University

Westminster Lodge

6. View of the central communal area.
The timber construction is left visible
so students can see how the building
was made.

7. Section.

8. Plan.

9. Despite its rustic appearance, the
interior is not dark. The glass rooflight
and generous windows ensure that
the building is flooded with daylight.

9

1. Site plan.
2. View across the site.

decided, with help from Architype, the softwood frames were erected and clad in standard-sized panels of Glasal and plasterboard. These were dry-fixed in a 'breathing wall' construction to eliminate the need for plastic vapour barriers. Thick layers of Warmcell recycled newspaper insulation in the walls and floors, and turf roofs sown with wild flowers, provide all the homes with excellent insulation. In addition, the window units were double-glazed and all windows have high-performance softwood frames. The system allows for most neighbourhood configurations. The Diggers residents chose a horse-shoe arrangement with the three-bedroom family houses raised up on stilts at the rear of the site, and the one-person flats grouped into two-flat units at the fore. The layout works well on the steeply sloping site. Each house or flat has a view from its south-facing conservatory and verandah (the family houses have two verandahs, one on each floor). Each home also has a generous porch looking on to communal gardens at the centre of the site. One of the residents' aims for the project was that it should be environmentally friendly and incorporate energy-saving measures. This was one reason why wood was chosen as the main building material. All the timber is from renewable sources and non-toxic paints and stains were used. The development exceeds current UK energy-saving targets. Thick insulation, double-glazing and south-facing conservatories keep energy bills down to an impressively low figure.

Most of the buildings in this chapter were designed by architects and built by skilled contractors. The Diggers self-build housing is the exception. Set on the outskirts of Brighton, its nine homes (five family houses and four flats for single people) were designed and built by the people who now live there, none of whom initially had any building skills. Working as a cooperative, they used a conceptually elegant timber-frame system which was developed by Architype and tailored to the group's requirements. User participation is an important strand of 'green' thinking. Because the labour is given free, self-build homes are significantly cheaper to construct than regular houses, enabling people to own a home who might not otherwise have been able to. In the process, self-builders learn a skilled trade. Architype's self-build system draws heavily on the Segal Method. This pioneering self-build housing system was developed in the 1970s by Walter Segal, the British architect of Swiss birth. (Architype partner Jon Broome worked with Segal before leaving to set up his own practice.) As with the ingenious Segal Method housing, Architype's self-build system uses a simple post-and-beam construction, non-load-bearing walls set out on a grid, and readily available materials. The Diggers residents worked together as a team, with the whole venture taking two years to complete. (The only professional input to the construction was the pouring of the concrete foundations.) Once the layout of each unit had been

17

Diggers self-build housing

Brighton, UK, 1996

Architype

3

Digger's self-build housing

3. Looking up the site to the two-storey family houses.

4. Ground-floor plan for a family house.

5. First-floor plan for a family house.

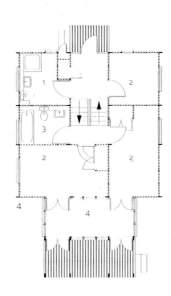

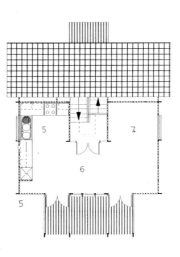

Digger's self-build housing
6. The homes form a horseshoe,
enclosing a communal garden.
7. Plan for the single person units.

key
1 bedroom
2 porch
3 hall
4 boxroom
5 bathroom
6 kitchen/dining
7 living
8 conservatory
9 verandah

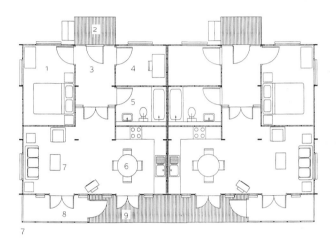

7

6

Digger's self-build housing
8. Section through a family house.
9. View of a living room in a family house with the conservatory and verandah beyond.
10. Conservatories provide buffered warm zones, which help to keep heating bills down.

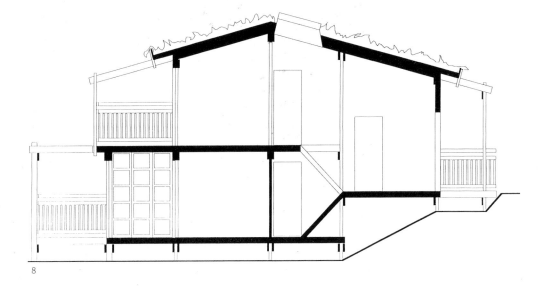

8

9

Digger's self-build housing
Architect: Architype
Robin Hillier, Jonathan Hines and Jon Broome
Structural engineer: Architype
Quantity surveyor: Architype
Contractor: Digger's Self-Build Co-op

This chapter looks at wooden buildings that have consciously been constructed as part

of the landscape in which they are sited. Existing hand-in-hand with the natural environ-

ment, the pleasure in these structures derives from the conjuring up of nature into the

interior space through decks, terraces, sliding windows and folding walls. These archi-

tects have indulged in the sensuality of wood: its warmth, fragrance and solidity.

RELATING TO NATURE

1

As with the previous chapter, the thread that links the buildings shown over the next few pages is the desire for a more environmentally responsive architecture. The practices whose work is shown are not, however, what is commonly understood by the term 'green' architects; while their work at times embraces some of the principles of environmental design – passive energy systems, environmentally friendly materials and so on – this is not its principal focus or *raison d'être*. Instead of resorting to technical fixes, their work appeals at an altogether more subtle level, by heightening the appreciation and aware-ness of nature through an architecture that deliberately engages with the natural world.

Sitting on the deck of the Israel House (pages 148–153) overlooking the Pittwa-ter basin, who could fail to be bowled over by the beauty of the Australian land-scape? A week away from it all at the Atlantic Arts Center (pages 160–167), deep in heart of Florida's jungly swamps, would make anyone appreciate the power of nature and its ability to put us back 'in touch' with ourselves.

Increased environmental awareness will never be achieved simply by harangu-ing people with tales of doom and gloom. There has to be an upside to the argu-

1. Woodlea Primary School,
Hampshire County Architect's
Department.
2. Lappish Civic Centre, Bjerk & Bjørge.
3. Summer house, Per Friberg.

2

ment or no one will bother with measures to help safeguard the planet's natural resources. Building is, of course, one of mankind's most damaging pursuits, accounting for the destruction of massive swathes of countryside each year. And yet buildings like the Israel House and Atlantic Arts Center, together with the others shown in this chapter, help us to appreciate the natural world by stepping out into the landscape with decks and terraces and inviting the landscape inside through huge sliding windows and folding walls.

The fact that these buildings are all made of wood is no coincidence. Like stone and mud, wood is a naturally available building material, part of the landscape itself. But whereas stone and mud are cold, dead and cool, wood has a warm, living sensuality. Beautiful to look at and soft and warm to the touch, wood is naturally fragrant, and sounds solid. Appealing to four of our five senses, perhaps part of its attraction is the subconscious links it sets up to the world around us – reminders of the smell of the forest, the feel of a smooth old tree and so on.

The protective light wood tar on the cladding of the Lappish Civic Centre (pages 180–185) heats up in the warmth of the summer sun, giving the pine building

a rich, aromatic smell. The Israel House's beeswax-polished walls and floor smell warm and pungent in the Australian heat. The solid pine floors of Per Friberg's summer house by the sea (pages 168–173) feel smooth and soft underfoot. Woodlea Primary School (pages 154–159) sounds solid and reassuring as children clatter about. What other building material is so alive, so intimately connected to the landscape around us and connecting us so well with it?

3

1. North elevation.
2. The approach to the house.

post-and-beam structure, stiffened by steel cleat connections. The two primary rafters of the curving roof are steel, supported on steel struts. The ground and first floor are clad, on three elevations, in panels of fibre cement sheeting; the externally hung sliding doors and windows are made from western red cedar and bluegum (a kind of eucalyptus). Above ceiling height the upper sleeping area is entirely glazed. The south façade is completely clad in kiln-dried vertical boarding of blackbutt, a durable Australian timber. The secondary structure of joists and studs is kiln-dried blond Victorian ash, a plantation timber chosen for its low shrinkage. External decking is in durable tallowwood, similarly chosen for its low shrinkage and because it comes from renewable plantations. Stutchbury likens the Israel House to an oyster, with its tough, crusty shell protecting a delicate interior. Inside, the house glows warm and soft. The walls and floor are lined in flooded gum, a pinkish, richly coloured plantation timber. Sealed in plant-based Livos oils and beeswax, the walls and floor not only glow, they also smell fragrant. All polished, the house provides a cosy retreat when the weather is bad. When it is good, the building opens up to the landscape. Doors and windows can be slid right open and the glass clerestory brings in light and provides views out over the treetops. The result is that while the Israel House has a vertical, thrusting form, its surroundings pervade the interior.

'In this country we have the rare opportunity to wander alone on a bush track, to be aware of hills and creeks and bush, and to feel emotions apart from the known, civilized ones,' explains Australian architect Peter Stutchbury. 'Our buildings should take in this opportunity to be able to "wander" in their surroundings.' While many of Stutchbury & Pape's buildings do just this, the house that was built for graphic designer Ken Israel does not so much wander through the bush as pop up out of it. Set on Sydney's northern peninsula, in the hills overlooking Pittwater, the Israel House is so intimately connected to its environment that it appears to take root in the rocky landscape. Its timber frame rises three storeys, in amongst the tree-canopy, and is capped off with a simple umbrella-like corrugated steel roof, curved and oversailing to follow the line of the hills and the path of the sun. The house is attractively simple. Like a grown-up tree house it essentially has just three rooms, each piled on top of the other. The lower-ground level is the utility area, housing the laundry and bathroom. Above is the living room, topped off with the main bedroom. Each room has large sliding windows on three sides, opening up to the elements. A bay running up the south elevation holds the kitchen, storage and toilet. Construction is not entirely in timber. The lower-ground floor has a solid concrete core which acts as bracing for the house. From this rises the tallowwood timber

18

The Israel House

Pittwater, Sydney, Australia

1994

Stutchbury & Pape Architects

1

2

3

The Israel House
3. West elevation. The house seems
to grow directly out of the rocky
landscape.
4. Half-hidden among the trees, the
house has spectacular views down
over the Pittwater marina.

4

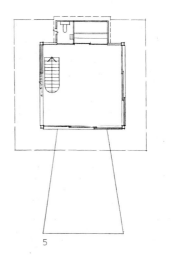

5

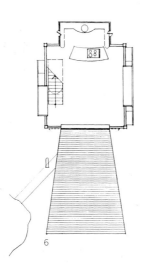

6

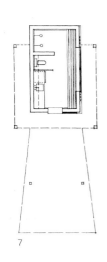

7

8

5. Second-floor level. Main bedroom with en suite bathroom.
6. First-floor level. Entry level with kitchen and living room.
7. Ground-floor level. Bathroom and utility room.
8. Lined in native Flooded gum, the first-floor living room and kitchen glow warm and smooth.
9. The oversailing curved roof acts as an umbrella, protecting the house from both rain and heat.
10. When the weather is fine, large sliding windows open the house up to its surroundings.

9

The Israel House
Architect: Peter Stutchbury
Project team: Ken Israel,
Peter Stutchbury, Jeff Broadfield,
Liam Flood, Nook Witzand
Engineer: Eva Tihany

10

1. Typical cross-section with classrooms opening out to the landscape and central circulation corridor.
2. View of the school in the landscape.

bowl. The building's composite structure reflects its relationship with the landscape. Brick walls and concrete floors are used at the rear of the site, where it cuts into the slope; where it opens out to the grassy bowl it is timber-framed with Douglas fir posts, laminated timber beams, load-bearing hardwood screens, softwood sections and wood decks. The building has shingle-covered roofs, which are pitched above the classroom wings and flat over the shared areas. The exception is the roof of the school hall which, being a much larger volume, has an asymmetrical portal frame of laminated timber. Most of the building is clad in shiplap boarding stained in a range of eleven earth-coloured natural pigments. Inside, the school is warm and light and full of child-focused details such as low-level sills on the windows, and low partition screens made of brick. The plan would suggest that the library at the heart of the building should be the school's social hub; the real focus of the interior, however, is its relationship with the outdoors. The design of the building encourages children to use the landscape around as a learning resource. Each classroom has a small, covered outside work space and shared decks that step down into the bowl. Five years after Woodlea swept the board of architectural prizes, a journalist revisited the school and found both teachers and pupils as enthusiastic as ever. The acting head teacher summed up the general mood when she said: 'I feel very special every day I come to work in this building.'

The designers of Woodlea Primary School – an internationally acclaimed local authority architect's department – won numerous awards when the building first opened. It is not hard to see why. Unlike the majority of local authority school buildings in the UK, which more often than not are bleak rectilinear boxes surrounded by a sea of black tarmac playground, this building forms an integral part of the children's learning experience. It is a child-friendly environment, organic in appearance and with an intimate relationship with the natural landscape around it. The building sits in a historic woodland site not far from an iron age fort. Although the ground slopes steeply, the architects chose not to simply level it flat. Instead they positioned the school at the edge of a natural bowl, placing it at the top (west) end of the site. A flat playing field was created lower down. This is linked to the school building by a narrow grassy swathe that cuts through the trees, ensuring that you never see the full extent of the cleared woodland. The main school building has an informal layout, arranged in a loose c-shape on three levels around the edges of the bowl. At one level is a central hub, housing common spaces such as the main entrance, the circulation areas and the library; the main hall, together with the music, drama and administration spaces, are grouped behind and above it. The classrooms are arranged in two spurs below the hub; each classroom has decks which open up to the grassy slope at the heart of the

19

Woodlea Primary School

Bordon, Hampshire, UK, 1991

Hampshire County Architect's

Department

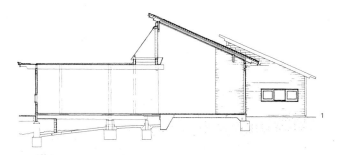

Woodlea Primary School
3. Plan.
4. Finished model.
5. The school is engulfed by the landscape.

key
1 infant class
2 junior class
3 library/resources
4 infant library
5 hall
6 decks
7 kitchen
8 waiting
9 main entrance
10 the bowl
11 outside work/play

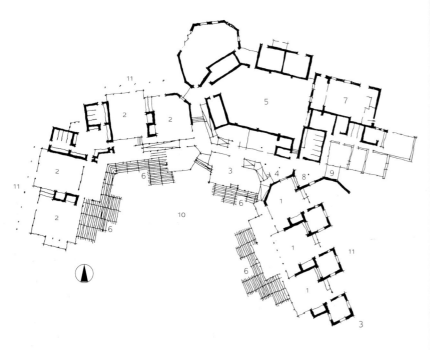

4

5

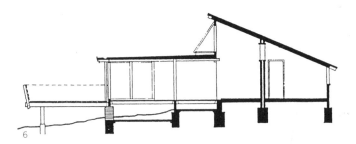

6

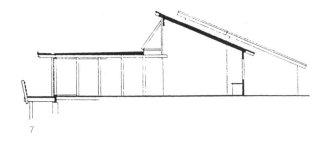

7

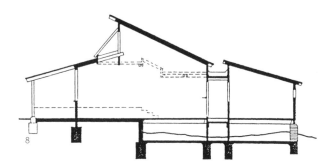

8

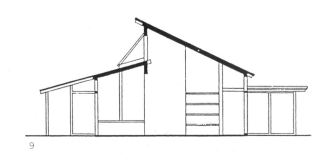

9

10

Woodlea Primary School

6–9. Various sections through the building.

10. Decks extend each classroom out into the landscape.

11. The main school hall with its asymmetric laminated timber portal frame.

12. Cross-section through the main school hall.

13. The school has a casual and informal quality.

Woodlea Primary School
Project architects: Nev Churcher,
Sally Daniels
Structural engineer: Watkinson and
Partners: Michael Wharf
Quantity surveyor: Dadson and Butler

11

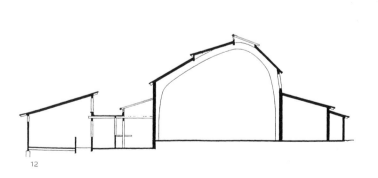

12

13

1. View of the music studio (left) and the painting studio (right). Windows are brushed aluminium, the doors are of steel and wood, and the roofs are finished in lead-coated copper.
2. The cedar boardwalk creates a serpentine path through the complex.

etation, their primary structure is a hardwood frame which is left exposed and clad in stained cypress. Inside, the buildings are clad in a hardwood-veneered plywood, horizontal cedar panelling and painted plasterboard. Each building houses a single activity and, although the basic structures are the same, each differs in its details. The music studio is deliberately insular: a box without windows. Daylight enters only through the large skylights, focusing attention on the work in hand. The dance studio has a window that looks on to vegetation on one side, as well as a ring of sandblasted windows 3.5 metres (15 feet) above the floor; the result is that light floods into the space without there being distracting views out. The painting studio, meanwhile, has high-level windows and three tall lightscoops on the roof. Topped off with glass and with louvres down their sides, these diffuse the light coming into the space and, by stack effect, ventilate the air-conditioned studio and avoid it becoming filled with paint fumes. One of Thompson & Rose's inspirations for the project was the architecture of other hot, tropical areas, hence the lightscoops and the studios' southern overhangs. The buildings highlight the weather patterns across the site. Light, wind and convection currents are integral to the way the studios work. In this way, residents on the various programmes do not only live in the dense vegetation; they also live with it.

Cut off by swampy creeks and overgrown with twisted scrub oaks, pine forest and palmetto bushes, New Smyrna Beach is the perfect retreat. Every year musicians, painters, sculptors, dancers and actors gather here at the Atlantic Center for the Performing Arts where, away from the distractions of everyday life, they focus on their work in a series of artist-in-residence programmes. The design of the Center is key to this sense of 'getting away from it all'. The six buildings which form the main creative studio spaces were designed by the young American husband-and-wife team, Maryann Thompson and Charles Rose. Their work generally combines strong geometric shapes with an interest in landscape architecture. At the Atlantic Arts Center, the result is a striking series of bold forms half-hidden in the thick vegetation. Because the studios are secluded, residents are able to concentrate exclusively on their work. Not that the centre is a solitary place – far from it. The boardwalks between buildings provide perfect opportunities for chance meetings and, because of the way the units are laid out, there is always the sense that some other activity is happening just around the corner. The design of the six studios is fairly simple. With the exception of the sculpture studio (which, because it houses heavy machinery and sculptures, has a poured concrete floor and boardmarked concrete walls), the studios are largely timber. Raised up on concrete piers above the dense veg-

20

Atlantic Center for the

Performing Arts

New Smyrna Beach, Florida,

USA, 1997

Thompson & Rose Architects

1

key

1 black box theatre
2 gallery/reception
3 dance studio
4 dressing room

5 sculpture studio
6 outdoor work area
7 painting studio
8 audio room
9 music room

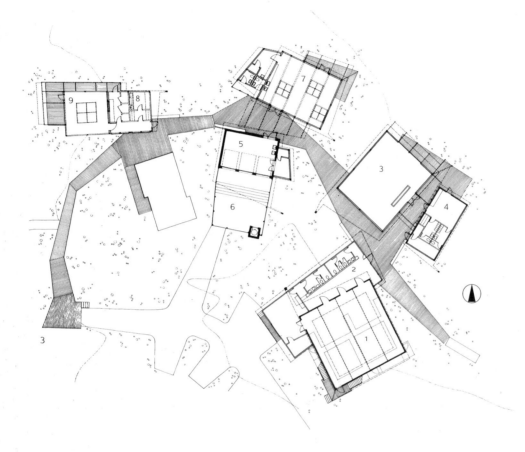

**Atlantic Center for the
Performing Arts**
3. Site plan.
4. Aerial view of the site almost hidden
from view in the swamps.
5. View of the painting studio
illuminated at night, with lightscoops
prominent.

6

**Atlantic Center for the
Performing Arts**

6. Music studio.
7. Although each building differs
in form, they belong to a common
morphology.
8. The music and painting studios.
9. Inside the painting studio.

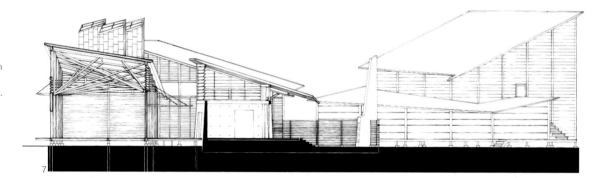

7

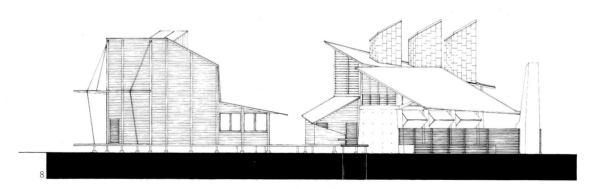

8

11

Atlantic Center for the Performing Arts

10 + 11. Exterior and interior of the library.
12. The sculpture studio and yard.
13. The sculpture and music studios.

Atlantic Center for the Performing Arts

Architects: Thompson and Rose
Architects, Cambridge, Massachusetts
Project designers: Charles Rose and
Maryann Thompson
Project team: Michael Grant,
Joseph MacDonald, Warren Van Wees,
Michael Breau, Francisco Thebaud,
Carrie Alice Johnson, Frank Dill,
Patrick Maguire, Lisa Iwamoto,
Michael Rose, Tim Downing
Client: Leeper Studio Complex,
Atlantic Center for the Arts; Ted Potter,
Former Executive Director;
Suzanne Tetscher, Current Executive
Director
Structural engineers: Ocmulgee
Associates
Civil engineers: Jerry K. Finley
Mechanical and electrical engineers:
M-Engineering
Geotechnical engineers: PSI-Jammal
Associates
Acoustical engineers: Cambridge
Acoustical
Construction manager: Epoch
Properties

12

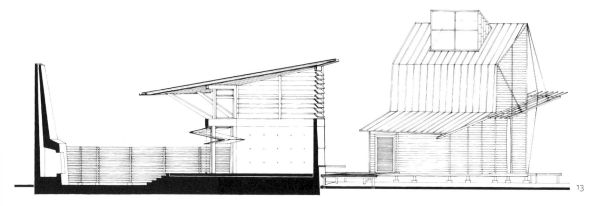

13

1. Site plan.
2. Rear elevation overlooking private garden.

Friberg builds in a range of materials, often choosing brick and stone. This house, however, uses wood – mainly oak, in an obvious reference to the forest around. Rough, unplaned 10 cm (4 inch) overlapping oak boards clad the front elevation. Horizontal 1.6 x 6.3cm ($^5/_8$ x 2 $^1/_2$ inch) ship-lap boarding lines the more sheltered garden elevation. Inside, the walls are lined with pale birch plywood, giving them a light and airy feel that contrasts with the more solid pine floors and tongue-and-groove ceiling. As the exterior timbers weather, the contrast between the tough outside world and the warm, smooth interior will become more pronounced. Inside, the rooms are oriented according to the sun's path. Three bedrooms connect in a suite on the building's east side. The dining room and kitchen are in the centre with the large living room to the west side, located to catch the last rays of the low Nordic sun. The layout, again, links inside and out. Access to the bedrooms is from outside, via an external deck (although the rooms also interconnect so that, in bad weather, you can walk from one to another). When the Fåglarö house was nominated for the Swedish Timber Prize in 1996, the jury commented: 'A feeling for the conditions of life in summer is expressed elegantly and self-evidently.' It is hard not to concur. The house has an inviting, open quality that makes the most of Sweden's endless summer days.

The interpenetration of nature and buildings is a key theme in Per Friberg's work. Trained as both landscape designer and architect, Friberg has been a dominant figure in his native Sweden since the 1950s, well known for a wide range of work that encompasses large landscape documentation projects, small gardens for single-family houses, and new-build villas. But perhaps his most evocative work remains the string of summer houses that he has designed throughout his career, of which the house in Fåglarö is one of the most recent examples. Fåglarö is one of the islands that make up Stockholm's inner archipelago. The scenery is spectacular: a jagged coastline of tiny inlets and rocky outcrops and, inland, historic woods and little development. It was here that Friberg's clients found their site: a south-facing spit of land 100 metres (320 feet) wide, surrounded on three sides by water and heavily wooded with pines and ancient oaks. The house sits in the middle of the site, thus leaving the coastline unspoilt and affording views in all directions. Its almost semicircular shape reflects the panoramic view and helps the house 'invite in' the natural surroundings: like a ripe fruit, the building's 'skin' appears to be split and interpenetrated by nature. Visitors arriving at the main entrance see right through the building to the landscaped garden beyond. Sheltered verandahs, decks and porches at the front and rear extend the house into nature.

21

Summer house

Fåglarö, Stockholm, Sweden

1993

Per Friberg

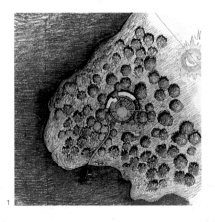

Summer house

3. Deck stepping out to the water.

4. Plan.

5. Front elevation. The curving plan ensures all rooms receive maximum natural light.

6. View of the rear elevation in amongst trees.

3

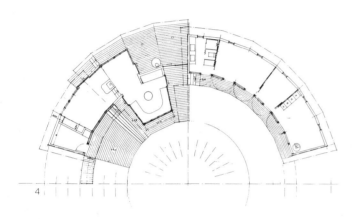

4

5

6

Summer house

7. Rear elevation.
8. Front elevation.

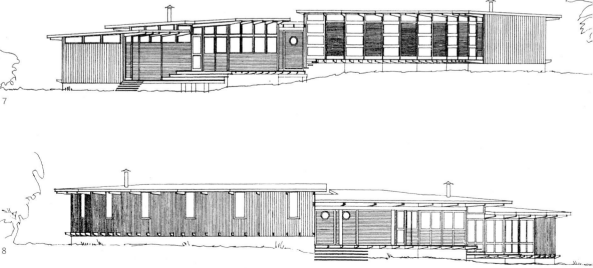

7

8

Summer house

9. Cross-section through bedroom.
10. Kitchen and outdoor eating area.
11. View of the bedrooms leading on
to each other.
12. Each bedroom opens out on to the
external deck.

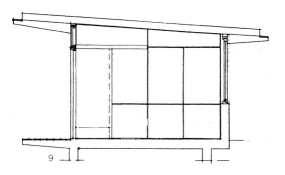

9

10

11

Summer house
Architect: Professor Per Friberg
Arkitekt SAR
Structural engineer: Civilingeniör
Gunnar Altenhammar
Quantity surveyor: ÅF Energikonsult
Landscape architect: Per Friberg

12

1. West elevation.
2. View of the nave looking east towards the altar.

structure to the site.' Making the most of its dramatic perch, the chapel soars as high as 26 metres (85 feet). It is a beacon in the landscape but, unlike most tall structures, it maintains a strong relationship with the ground thanks to a huge pitched roof which swoops virtually down to ground level, bringing the building visually 'down to earth'. Inside, the main architectural focus is the 37 metre (150 foot) long nave. This dramatic space is dominated by views of the building's soaring structure, an almost Gothic piece of craftsmanship. Made of Douglas fir (a material selected by the architects for its strength and availability), the structure was conceived of as a delicate piece of lace that would both help to pull the building together structurally and allow shafts of daylight through to illuminate the Chapel's interior spaces. The critical structural consideration when working with wood is always how to connect the pieces and transfer stresses across the connections. At Skyrose Chapel, a virtue has been made of necessity and the connections turned into one of the building's key features. The steel connecting pieces not only transfer and guide the forces in the structure, they also become a kind of 'jewellery', highlighting the structure of the building. Below ground level, by contrast, the building is sober and plain. Running underneath the nave is a large mausoleum containing 1,000 crypts and 600 urn niches.

Since setting up his Arkansas-based practice in 1953, Fay Jones has developed a distinctive architectural style. His buildings, which tend to be constructed of wood, have an almost spiritual relationship with their settings. 'We have always striven to place our buildings so that they are of the landscape, not on the landscape', explains partner Maurice Jennings, who has been with the practice for twenty-five years. 'The building and landscape should maintain a symbiotic relationship where each gains from the association.' In this, the practice's approach has been deeply influenced by the work of Frank Lloyd Wright, under whom Fay Jones studied on a Taliesin fellowship. Wright's style can be seen in the formal language of many of their buildings as well as, more loosely, in the spirit of their work and its relationship to nature – Wright liked to refer to nature as 'Nature spelled with a capital "N", the way you spell God with a capital "G".' There are other influences too: the works of American crafts-style architects Greene and Greene and organicist Bruce Goff are cited by Jennings as key to the development of the practice's approach. Skyrose Chapel is typical of their recent work. Situated on the slope of a mountain overlooking the Los Angeles basin and the Catalina Islands, the Chapel forms part of the Rose Hills Memorial Park and is used for weddings and funerals as well as occasional concerts. 'Of prime importance,' says Jennings, 'is the relationship of the

22

Skyrose Chapel

Whittier, California, USA, 1997

Fay Jones and Maurice Jennings

Architects

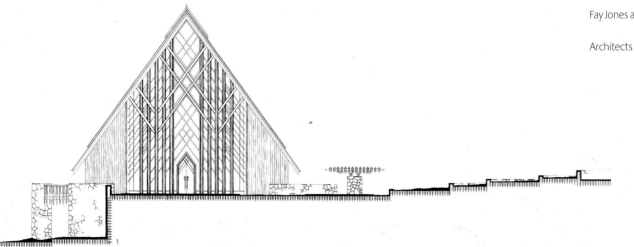

Skyrose Chapel

3. West elevation showing the church soaring up in the landscape.

4. South elevation, showing rooflights and side windows that illuminate the interior.

5. Ground-floor plan.

key

1 flower display
2 ceremonial
3 nave
4 narthex
5 clergy
6 family
7 waiting
8 office
9 preparation
10 robing
11 women
12 men

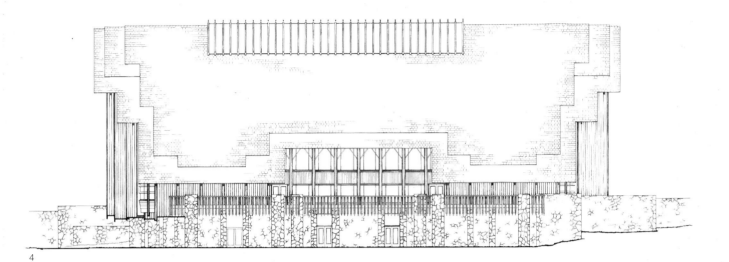

4

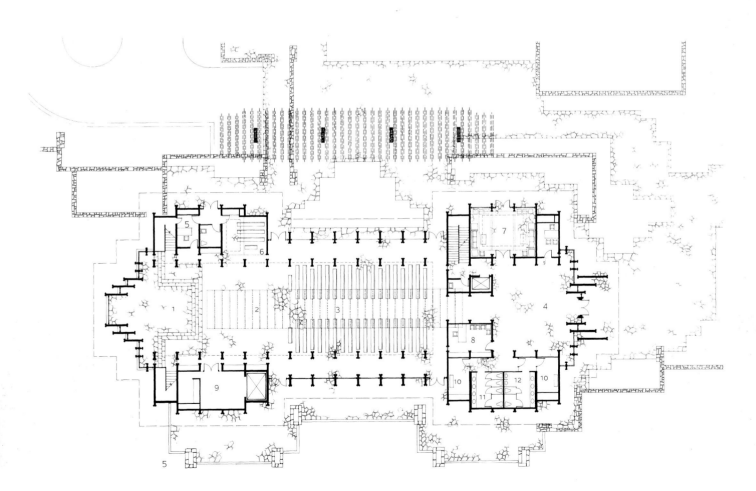

5

Skyrose Chapel

6. The gallery level, looking west. The nave is to the left.

7. View from the nave looking up at the highly Gothic roof structure, an intricate lattice of wood and glass.

8. Long cross-section.

9. Short cross-section showing the mausoleum below.

7

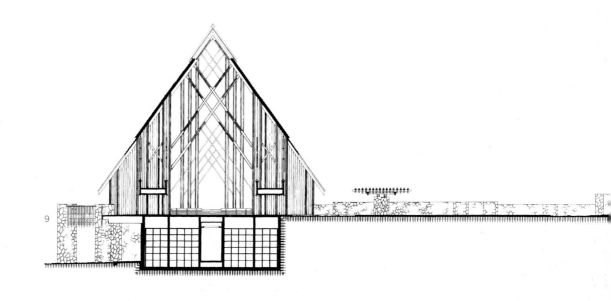

8

9

Skyrose Chapel

Architect: Fay Jones and
Maurice Jennings Architects
Project team: Fay Jones,
Maurice Jennings, David McKee,
Barry McNeill, Ted Jones,
Lancer Livermont, Bradley Edwards,
Jason Hayes
Structural engineer: Taylor and Gaines
Builder: Pozzo Construction,
Vic Pozzo
Superintendent: Gene Wilcott

1. Side elevation.
2. Close-up of the main entrance.

concourse. Opening on to it are workshops and outlets used by Lappish crafts-men to make and sell their silver, textiles, knives and stonework. At the east end of the building is a café and the auditorium or *lavvu*, currently used as the seat of the Lappish parliament. Bjørge wanted to use local pine, from forests in the Karasjok area, but Scandinavian pine proved cheaper. The roof structure is of laminated wood, clad in silver-coloured aluminium and zinc. The structure of the walls is left exposed and the cladding treated in a light wood tar that helps protect it from the ravages of winter and gives the building a fragrant smell in summer. This dark colouring contrasts with the external canopy, which is treated in a clear wood oil. The client, the municipality of Karasjok, initially asked for a building in Lappish style when they commissioned Bjerk & Bjørge. Some of the windows are picked out in red, yellow and blue: the Lappish colours. Beyond this, however, little attempt has been made to give the building a traditional appearance. Bjørge successfully argued that there is no real tradition of Lappish building. In nomadic culture what matters, he says, is not so much how buildings are constructed, as how the land is used. The civic centre provides them with a facility that, opening up in a grand sweeping curve towards the land, relates to the landscape that is their heritage, uses traditional building materials and provides them with the spaces necessary to continue their indigenous crafts.

For the Lapps, the far reaches of the Scandinavian outback are not a romantic option but a gruelling way of life. The Lapps (or Sami, as they call themselves) are traditionally an itinerant people, wandering the most northerly reaches of Scan-dinavia. Bjerk & Bjørge's civic centre at Karasjok, the Lapps' Norwegian capital, provides them with a meeting and trading base and, while their new parliament building is being constructed, a temporary political centre. Karasjok is high in the arctic circle, and conditions are extreme. For two months in midwinter the sun does not rise above the horizon. In the perpetual dark, temperatures can drop as low as minus 40 degrees centigrade. High summer, in contrast, brings constant sunshine and comparative warmth (typically 20 degrees centigrade). Building in these conditions is, of course, difficult; construction must be swift to achieve enclosure before the onset of winter, and materials have to be both durable and able to withstand the temperature fluctuations. For both reasons, says architect Eilif Bjørge, the partnership chose to design the civic centre entirely in wood. Sited on the outskirts of the settlement, the c-shaped complex of buildings defines the edge of the open market square. The main elevation faces the square and is marked by a curved canopy which is cantilevered off wood columns, creating a sense of welcome at the same time as affording real protection from the elements. Inside, the building features a continuous wide

23

Lappish Civic Centre

Karasjok, Norway, 1990

Bjerk & Bjørge

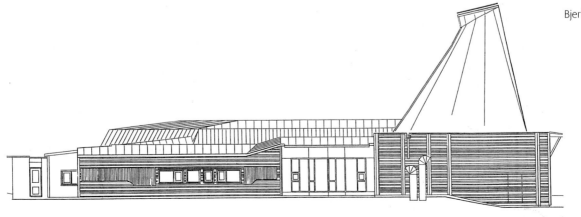

3

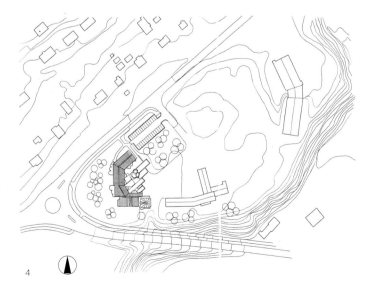

4

Lappish Civic Centre
3. View of the front elevation with the
curving cantilevered canopy.
4. Site plan.
5. Plan.

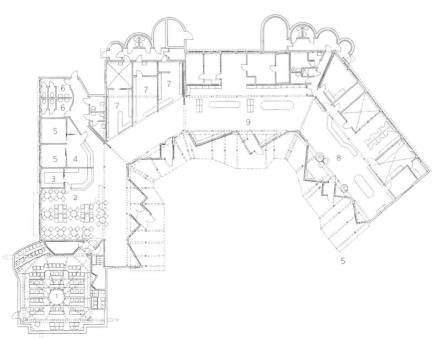

key

1 auditorium
2 café
3 kitchen
4 information
5 office
6 wcs
7 craft workshops
8 silversmith
9 sale and production of Lappish
  handicrafts

6

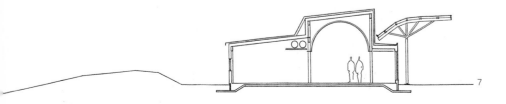

7

Lappish Civic Centre

6. Shops and workshops open off the main concourse.

7. Cross-section through the Lappish Civic Centre.

8 + 9. Sections through meeting chamber.

10. Meeting area and cafeteria.

11. Interior view of the auditorium.

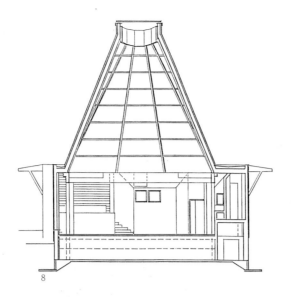

8

10

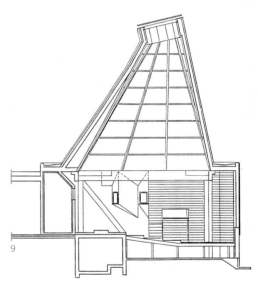

9

Lappish Civic Centre
Architect: Bjerk og Bjørge as MNAL, NPA,
Bergen, Eilif Bjørge (architect), Kari Ulla
(interior architect)
Structural: Siv. ing Bjørn Vileid MRIF,
Tromsø
Ventilation: Siv. ing Asbjørn Sletten,
MRIF, Vadsø
Electrical: IGP as, Alta

11

1. The house that Starck built for himself.
2. Verandahs surround the house so that it seems to spread out into the landscape.

Philippe Starck has houses all over the world. But his favourite, he claims, is his French base, a timber-framed house in the countryside outside Paris. Far from being the one-off architectural showpiece you expect of an internationally renowned designer, the house is one that anyone with a plot of land and £144,000 ($240,000) could build. Starck's home is a kit house, created by him for the French mail-order company, 3 Suisses. To build it you buy a £600 ($1,000) box from the company which contains a handbook; plans giving estimates of the materials needed; a video showing construction techniques; a hammer; a notebook; a watercolour to hang on the finished walls, and a French flag (it is apparently traditional in France to fly a flag over newly completed houses). The manufacturers estimate that it should take around two months to build the house, at a cost of £106,000 ($176,000) without verandah, or £144,000 with, not including the price of the land. Starck says he designed the kit house with low-income families specifically in mind: 'I was irked by the tragedy of people who pore over glossy home-decoration magazines, but who can never fulfil that dream because their income confines them to a choice of anonymous and degenerate housing.' It is, however, difficult to see the house as a solution to mass housing needs. Essentially a rural – or at best suburban – dwelling, it is, as Starck himself has said, 'the house that everyone subconsciously dreams of owning', an idyllic

retreat from the built-up city life that the majority will always endure. The main building material is wood, partly because of its low cost, but also because it permits a high degree of flexibility, allowing mistakes to be rectified or rooms to be added at a later stage. The type of wood is left to the customer – almost any softwood would work. Precise construction details are only available to those who buy the kit. All Starck says is that anyone, with a bit of help from a professional builder, should be capable of putting the house together as they want. In Starck's version of the house the walls and roof are largely glazed, but again this can be altered to suit particular requirements. The plan is similarly flexible. The two-storey house can have just one very large bedroom or up to four smaller ones. These are located on the upper floor together with the bathroom(s). Downstairs, Starck suggests an open-plan living area with kitchen and separate cloakroom and scullery. The wrap-around verandah, supported on log posts, provides an extension to the ground-floor living area and extends the house into the country-side around. The 3 Suisses company will not reveal how many kits it has sold. One suspects that the project was more a profile-raising exercise than a serious venture into the building trade (certainly the promise of kit houses by other leading designers has not materialized). Nevertheless, Starck's house exists, and anyone with the land and cash to spare could, in theory, build their own rural idyll.

24

3 Suisses kit house

Rambouillet Forest, France

1994

Philippe Starck

4

3 Suisses kit house
previous pages
3. Hidden in the Rambouillet Forest
outside Paris, Starck's house is a
rural idyll.

5

3 Suisses kit house
Architect: Philippe Starck
Project team: Patrick Bouchain, Loïc Julienne

6

3 Suisses kit house
4. Tree-like rough-hewn posts: a reminder of timber in its natural state.
5. First-floor bathroom and bedroom form a single room.
6. Ground-floor living space.

chapter five

Familiar idioms rooted in local culture, as shown here, provide a foil to some of the

more formal architecture in the book. Timber-framed and timber-clad, the ingenuity of

these very contemporary buildings is to sit effortlessly within their given environment.

Illustrating the way that the vernacular can provide new models by reworking traditional

forms, these buildings both harmonize with and respond to, everyday life.

VERNACULAR UPDATED

2

Today you can create a building almost any shape you want. Take just two examples, both of which opened in 1997: the Guggenheim Museum in Bilbao, Spain, and the Jewish Museum in Berlin, Germany. Designed on the computer that built the Mirage jet fighter, Frank Gehry's Guggenheim is a wildly expressionistic building in which no two pieces of its huge titanium-clad roof are the same shape. In Berlin, Daniel Libeskind has created an equally extraordinary form: a hybrid between a star of David and the lightning symbol of the German SS.

Extraordinarily sophisticated computer-aided design programs are helping to transform our idea of what buildings can look like. Certainly it is an exciting time to be designing, but one need not be an aesthetic reactionary to imagine that

some of the buildings of this period, like those of the 1960s before them, may, in years to come, be seen as the triumph of new ideas over content. Deep down there is something innately conservative about our reaction to buildings: people want homes and offices and public buildings with which they can engage on some level. One way of doing this, through the vernacular, is explored in this chapter.

Too often the vernacular is thought of as something stylistic, as a return to the forms of the past. But this is far from the truth. Vernacular buildings can look just as modern as any other; what distinguishes them is that they are in some way rooted in the local culture, giving them a resonance within their environment. As Canadian architect Brian Mackay-Lyons (whose LeGallais House is shown on pages 224–229) explains:

The vernacular ... is a process or cultural view, connected to the material culture and the culture of building. By taking up new technologies and materials the vernacular is always contemporary and forward-looking, rather than sentimental and backward-looking. For the architect to embrace the vernacular is by definition to accept the idea of convention. The conventional ways to make

1

things, the conventional sequences and methods of the building industry become the medium of the architect.

Wood is frequently the material of choice for vernacular buildings. It remains the traditional building material in much of the world, tends to be cheap, and is easy to work – attributes which combine to make it an ideally suited medium. The buildings shown in this chapter are all timber-framed, and most are also timber-clad, although Clare Design's Hammond House (pages 196–201) in Queensland, Australia, is finished in corrugated iron like the local barns on which it draws for inspiration.

One of the most significant projects to be shown is the Next Home (pages 236–239), designed by the architecture department at Canada's McGill University in response to the need for cheap and flexible housing to suit modern home owners. The house, with its traditional-looking façade but infinitely changeable interior, is a perfect illustration of how the vernacular can continue to provide new models by reworking traditional forms. The result is an architecture that at once fits in with other buildings and is continually responsive to changing patterns of living.

1. Hammond House, Clare Design.
2. LeGallais House, Brian MacKay-Lyons.
3. Japanese Pavilion at Expo '92, Tadao Ando Architect & Associates.

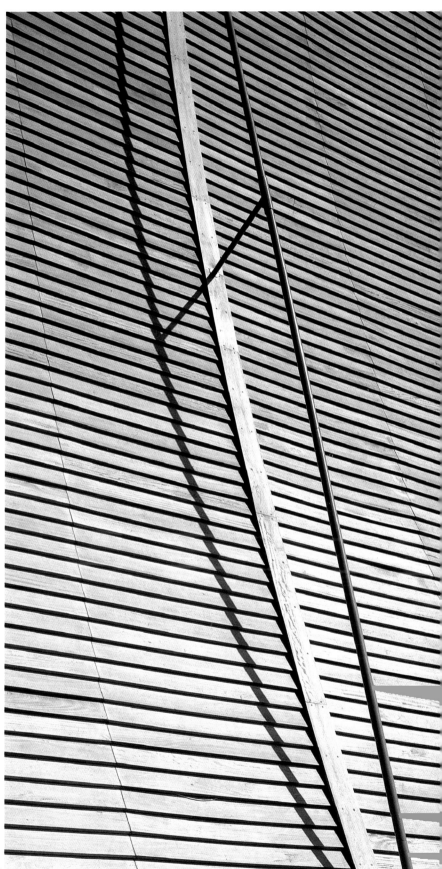

3

1 + 2. North elevation showing the
main entrance and outdoor deck.

vations. These are made of two sheets of local hoop pine plywood with an internal stud framing. Prefabricated gang nail trusses are connected to the top of the fins. This helps give the house sufficient rigidity to withstand the 60 metres per second/130 miles per hour cyclones that batter the site. While the east and west elevations are clad in corrugated iron, with large windows, the north and south walls are made from prefabricated plywood with an exposed frame. These are detailed without bottom plates to prevent rot in wet weather. The roof is clad inside with ply and outside with zincalumite which extends, like an apron, over the entire house, sheltering it from the elements. Store rooms and sheds cluster round the edges of the house; one stores the rainwater barrel, while another houses the solar energy storage batteries that provide all the power. The house is designed with climate and context in mind. It is tightly planned, laid out on a grid of six modules. The verandah, which occupies one module, leads into the open-plan living and eating areas. Sliding pine-board walls screen the bedroom and bathroom, providing privacy while maintaining the cross-ventilation, which is generated by louvred slats in the exterior walls. The building's relationship with the landscape is reinforced at a subliminal level by the use of local woods. Brims hoop pine ply and spotted gum are used for the interior lining and floor. These give the interior a warm glow and link it with the bush on to which it looks in three directions.

The inspiration upon which Lindsay and Kerry Clare draw is not a grand tradition but the everyday landscape of rural Queensland, with its simple corrugated iron-clad barns and outbuildings, and ramshackle timber-framed houses. The Hammond House takes its cue from this largely unnoticed architecture, transforming it into an elegant, lightweight structure. Set in the magnificent volcanic terrain of the hinterland north of Noosa, the Hammond House was designed for a semi-retired couple who wanted a self-sufficient, low-cost, low-maintenance cottage that would also take best advantage of the landscape they love. The house was largely prefabricated and assembled by a skilled craftsman on site. Clare Design decided on timber rather than steel for the main structural elements because steel fabrication and on-site welding is expensive and steel also tends to corrode in the harsh Queensland climate. Their kit design – a prototype, they hope, for others – acknowledges the Queensland practice of pre-cutting timber frames for houses. This practice is itself a response to the same problems of transport across difficult terrain and the need for rapid construction in remote locations. The foundation posts are treated ironbark, a very durable type of eucalyptus traditionally used in the area. These support 300 x 30mm (11 ¾ x 1 ¼ inch) bearers, also in iron-bark, that in turn support hardwood joists. From this floor platform, loads are taken by plywood fin-bracing walls running down the building's east and west ele-

25

Hammond House

Queensland, Australia, 1992

Clare Design

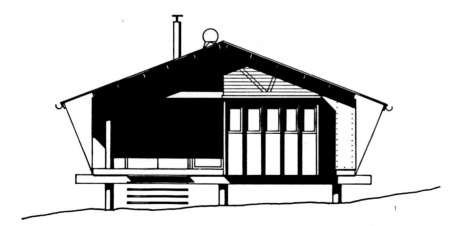

1

2

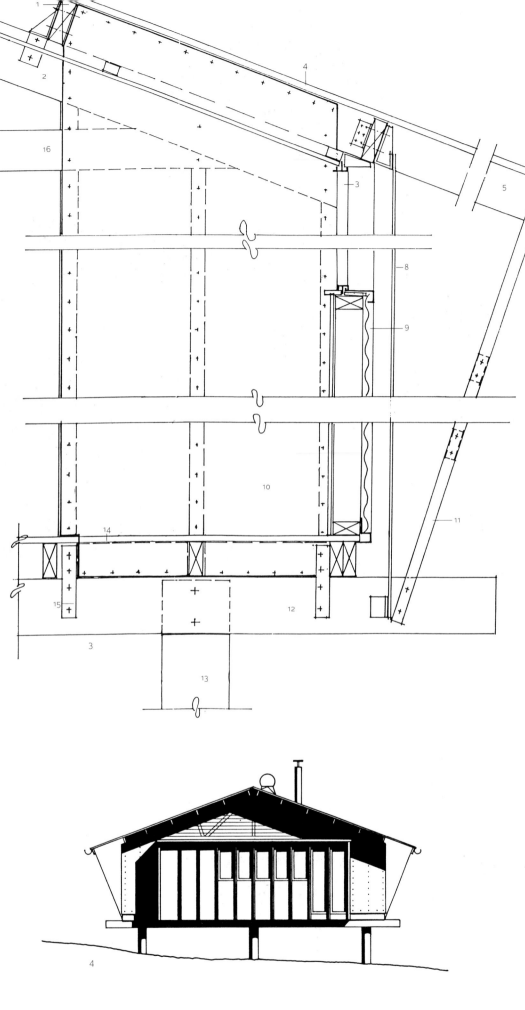

6

Hammond House

3. Construction drawing showing how the roof, wall and floor are detailed.
4. South elevation.
5. Detail showing the louvred glass slats that help cross-ventilation.
6. View of the house, adjoining carport and sheds in the landscape.
7. East elevation.

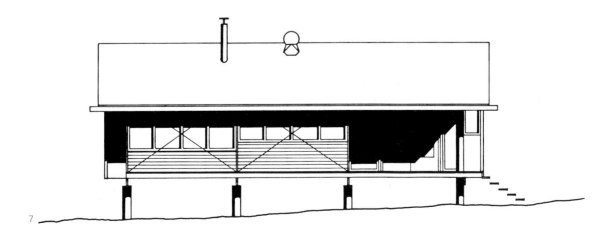

7

8

9

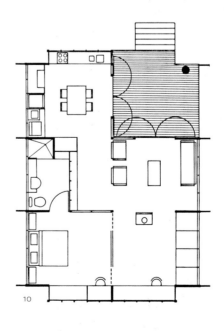

10

Hammond House

8. The main living room with its bracing fin walls and exposed gang trusses.

9. Corner detail. Built-in furniture helps to maximize the living space.

10. Plan.

11

Hammond House

11. Slatted sliding partitions separate off the bedroom while maintaining cross-ventilation.
12. View from the living room out to the deck which extends the building into the landscape.
13. Doors fold back so that the dining area opens up to the deck.
14. Cross-section.

Hammond House

Architect: Clare Design
Project team: Kerry Clare, Lindsay Clare
Structural engineer: McWilliam Consulting Engineers
Builder: Terry McLardy

13

12

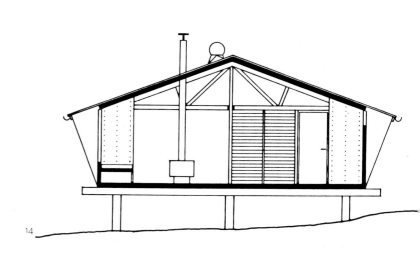

14

1. View from the street.
2. Rear elevation.

the original San Francisco development pattern. The choice of materials also appears to hark back to earlier San Francisco traditions. All buildings are made of Douglas fir, using straightforward construction techniques. Much low-density construction in the US is built from timber. However, Solomon says his choice was motivated more by the material's relative cheapness, and the speed at which timber frames can be erected, than by any ecological or historic motives. Amancio Ergina Village may on the outside recall the style of traditional developments, but internally the apartments are very different. The small kitchens, large dining areas and multiple bedrooms of the nineteenth century have given way to airy open-plan living. The one-, two- and three-bedroom apartments are compact, with minimal circulation; the resultant savings went on amenities such as decks, back stairs and small gardens. Each receives daylight from front and rear, and enjoys cross-ventilation. Kitchens are large and open on to the dining and living spaces. When the Californian chapter of the American Institute of Architects awarded the Village its First Honor award, the jury was effusive: 'This project reinforced San Francisco's urban form and context beautifully, with a slightly new vocabulary. Improvement such as better daylighting and security go far beyond the original townhouse structure, and amenities create a sense of community within the project ... Artistically, visually and socially, this architecture is very successful.'

Capturing the indefinable 'essence of place' is one of architect Daniel Solomon's preoccupations. Fascinated since the early 1970s by San Francisco's vernacular, he has studied the city's housing types in design studios at Berkeley University and the City Planning Department. Now running his own practice, specializing in housing and urban design work, Solomon tackles these issues in his built projects. Amancio Ergina Village is a development of 72 apartments built specifically for low- and moderate-income groups. The site was an urban renewal area which retained some vestiges of the original city structure and a number of rehabilitated nineteenth-century terraced houses. Solomon's reworking of the site succeeds in both recovering the city structure and relating to the existing houses, without resorting to pastiche. The scheme comprises a series of 15 metre (50 foot) blocks, each housing four or six apartments. The central portion of each building, measuring 7.5 metres (25 feet), is articulated with a pair of bays that flank the entrance. These serve as a reminder of the structure of the former terraced houses, which conformed to the same standard of measurement. These buildings are organized around the edge of the site, leaving the centre free for communal and private gardens. Each apartment has its own walk-up entrance plus a second entrance at the rear. Half-way down, the block is bisected by an alleyway overlooked by some of the apartments – another distinctive feature of

26

Amancio Ergina Village

San Francisco, USA, 1992

Daniel Solomon Architecture

and Urban Design

1

2

Amancio Ergina Village

3. The massing of the development reflects traditional San Francisco patterns.

4. View looking down towards the traditional housing on which the scheme is modelled.

3

4

5

Amancio Ergina Village
5. Front elevation.
6. Site plan.

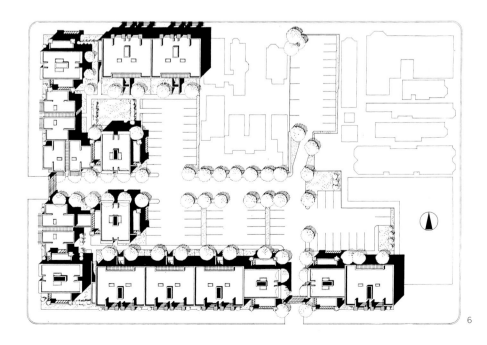

6

Amancio Ergina Village
7. The use of timber is a further link with traditional timber-frame housing.

7

Amancio Ergina Village
8. Numerous windows ensure well-lit
interiors and dynamic elevations.
9. Section through a wall.

8

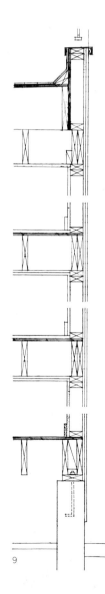

9

Amancio Ergina Village

10 + 11. Typical plans.
12. Each group of flats has its own entrance.
13. The development encloses private and communal gardens.
14 + 15. Typical plans.

key

1 living/dining
2 kitchen
3 bedroom
4 living room
5 dining room

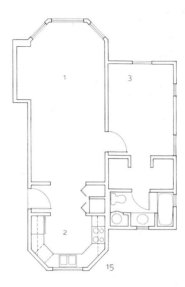

14

15

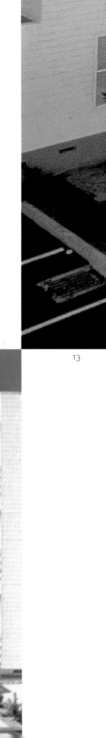

12

13

Amancio Ergina Village

Architect: Solomon Architecture and Urban Design
Daniel Solomon, Connie Giles, John Long
Structural engineer: Shapiro, Okino, Hom & Associates, San Francisco
Landscape architect: SWA Group, Sausalito

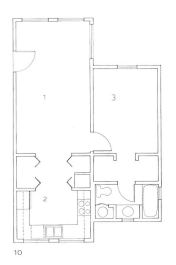

10

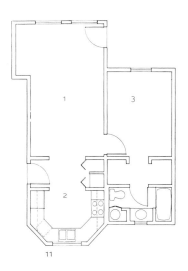

11

key
1 living/dining
2 kitchen
3 bedroom

1. End elevation.
2. Zorn is a modernization of local black- and red-painted vernacular buildings – as shown in this corner detail.

are mostly vertical but above the parapet, and in a few other small areas, they run parallel to the roof. The roof is made of laminated wooden beams with loose-fill insulation and an outer layer of zinc. The window joinery and planed timber is painted, in the Zorn tradition, in 'English red'. Large sliding shutters pull across the windows and entrance to ensure light does not damage the collection and to help protect the building during the winter months, when it is closed to the public. The building thus acquires something of the appearance of a sophisticated barn. The plan is fairly straightforward. Visitors enter a large reception area. To the left are staff areas, including the kitchen and staff room. The public parts of the building are to the right of the entrance hall. Here there is a large rectangular room, known as the textile chamber, in which most of the collection is displayed and stored. Movable screens conceal a store area. A set of doors leading off the chamber give on to the study room, which is also used for temporary exhibitions. In contrast to the museum's dark exterior, the interior finishes are light. The walls are covered in grey-painted sawn-faced wallboarding, the ceilings lined in white-tinted tongue-and-groove boards. In the main gallery spaces, the floors are finished in oiled boards, also tinted white. There is some colour in the entrance hall, which has a veined porphyry floor, but otherwise the tone is cool and neutral, leaving the brightly coloured materials on display to give life to the place.

Mora is a small town in central Sweden. Besides the ski resort, its primary attraction is the Gammerlgarden, a house built by the turn-of-the-century painter Anders Zorn. Zorn and his wife were keen social anthropologists, amassing a large collection of woven textiles, lace and costumes produced by local peasants. For most of this century their collection has remained under wraps in the Zorn Museum archive. In 1992, however, funding became available and Andersson + Landström were commissioned to design a purpose-built museum to house the collection. The task was not straightforward. Because of the fragile nature of the collection (many of the delicate textiles cannot withstand direct sunlight) the building required sophisticated daylight and humidity controls. Despite the high-tech nature of the museum's environmental system, however, an avant-garde aesthetic would not have been suitable, being out of keeping with the adjacent Arts and Crafts-style Gammerlgarden and the Mora *timmerhus* tradition of clapboard houses. Andersson + Landström's museum is a modern reinterpretation of the clapboard vernacular. The resultant black- and red-painted timber building is an abstraction: the local tradition distilled down to a series of simple, sloping planes. The museum was built by local craftsmen who were assigned to the project by the employment office. Its construction comprises a framework of timber studs which are clad outside in sawn-finished boarding, stained black. The boards

27

Zorn Textile Museum

Mora, Sweden, 1994

Andersson + Landström

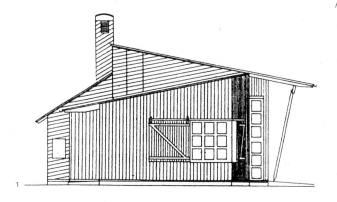

Zorn Textile Museum
3. Plan.
4. View from the approach.

key

1   reception area
2   cloakroom
3   kitchenette
4   staff room
5   staff entrance
6   services/distribution board
7   textile chamber
8   movable screens
9   store
10 study room/temporary exhibitions
11 store/ventilating equipment
12 refuse store

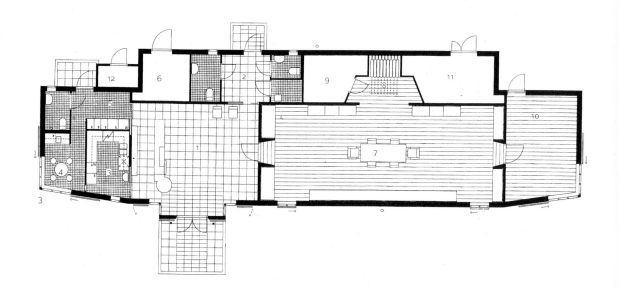

3

4

5

Zorn Textile Museum

5. End elevation. The sloping roofs
update the vernacular tradition.
6. Front elevation.
7. Rear elevation.

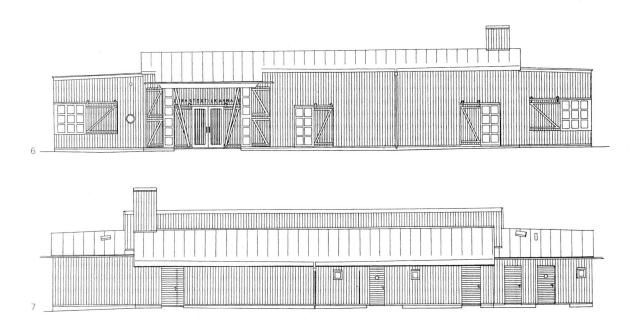

6

7

Zorn Textile Museum
8. The cloakroom.
9. Cross-section through entrance area.
10. Entrance area looking through to the textile chamber.
11. The exterior is deliberately barn-like with rough-hewn timbers and heavy, sliding shutters.

8

Zorn Textile Museum
Architect and landscape architect: Andersson + Landström AOS ARC AB Anders Landström
Assistant: Mikael Bergqvist
Structural engineer: Hans Hansson & Co., Kurt L. Rönlund

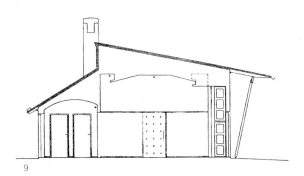

9

10

11

1. Site plan.
2. View looking down one of the rows
of terraced housing.

and run down the slope. Each house is set back from the path, and has a raised, semi-private garden that is shielded by a low, white-painted fence. Thus, despite the density of the housing programme, the individual dwellings have a high degree of privacy. The arrangement also means that even the east-facing houses have a sunny area in the afternoon. Inside, each house is largely open-plan on the ground floor. The small hallway opens up to a kitchen and dining room at the front. The living area is at the rear of the house, with views over the communal back gardens. Upstairs there are two bedrooms, one with a bathroom. Although all might appear fairly straightforward, considerable care has gone into the way the new houses relate to the existing village. Not only are they deliberately low in height, so as not to overwhelm the pre-existing houses, but also they pick up on traditional materials commonly used in the area. The development is nevertheless ultra-modern in its procurement. Each house is made up using an industrially prefabricated timber frame construction system, which employs load-bearing transverse walls. The timber walls and floor elements were brought ready-made to the site, assembled and then clad in wood shiplap boarding. The roofs were meanwhile covered in titanium zinc. This fast-track technique helped keep costs down by reducing the amount of time and skilled labour needed on site.

The Danish practice Tegnestuen Vandkunsten (often known just as Vandkunsten) has, over the past 25 years, built up a reputation for excellent low-cost social housing that, while providing innovative solutions to social problems, looks very much part of a north European tradition. It is a track record that in the early 1990s led to an invitation to take part in a German competition for timber-built rented housing, to cost not more than DM 1,800 per square metre, in Bavaria. Vandkunsten not only won three projects as a result of the contest, but it was also commissioned to design housing for a further two sites. One of these was at Rödental-Spittelstein, a village near Coburg, in eastern Germany. The site, not far from the heart of the old village, is a strip of land running down a slight hill to a road, with a beautiful wood on the other side. Vandkunsten organized the housing in five blocks; taking its cue from the site's topography, these are arranged as four strips (of 37 rented homes each) that follow the slope plus a fifth block (of seven privately owned houses) at the top of the site. The latter runs at right angles to the slope and forms a containing edge to the estate. A community hall on the northern edge of the site forms a landmark that holds the whole ensemble together visually. The hall provides a venue for events and room for storage, and also accommodates the heating plant for the entire complex. The houses are reached by two paths that lead off the central square

28

Housing in Rödental-

Spittelstein

near Coburg, Germany, 1996

Tegnestuen Vandkunsten

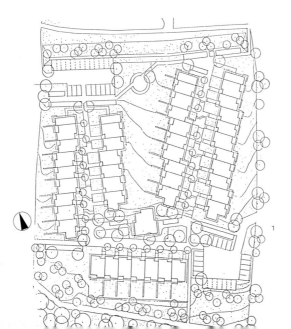

1

3

Housing in Rödental-Spittelstein
3. Aerial view.
4. View looking back up the slope and
at the gardens in front of each house.
5. The houses seen from the rear.
6 + 7. Elevations of the stepped-down
housing strip, garden face (6) and
entrance face (7).

4

5

6

7

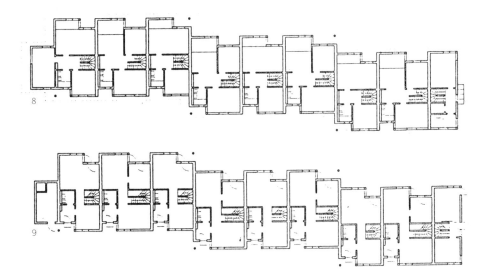

Housing in Rödental-Spittelstein
8. First-floor plan.
9. Ground-floor plan.

overleaf
10. General view of the site.

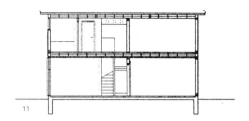

11

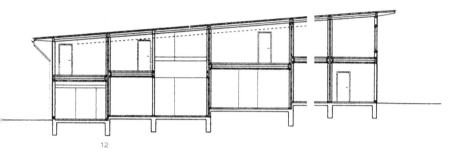

12

13

14

Housing in Rödental-Spittelstein
11 + 12. Typical cross-sections.
13. First-floor landing.
14. A typical living room.
15. Construction detail of the external and party walls.

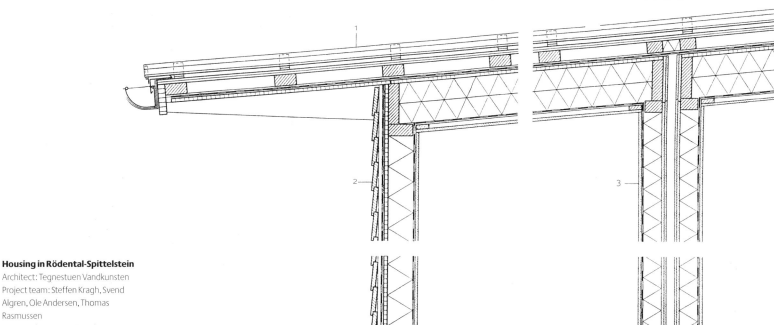

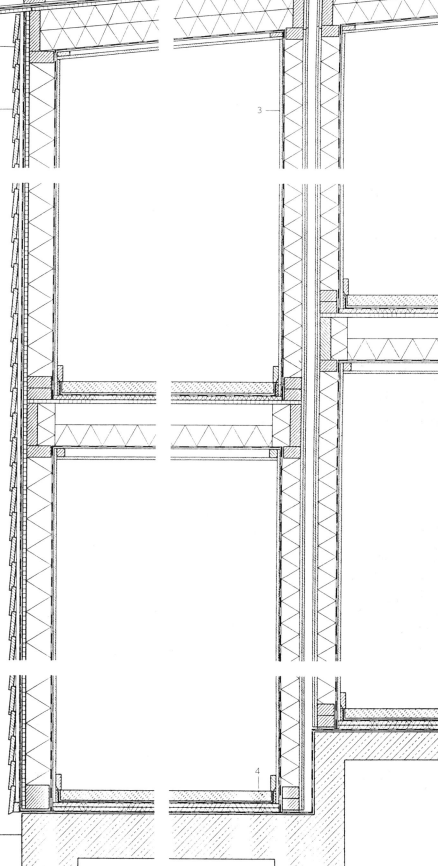

Housing in Rödental-Spittelstein

Architect: Tegnestuen Vandkunsten

Project team: Steffen Kragh, Svend Algren, Ole Andersen, Thomas Rasmussen

Structural engineer: IB Möbus, Nürnberg

Quantity surveyor: WBG Coburg

key

1 titanium-zinc sheet roofing
   24mm sawn tongue-and-groove boarding with sound absorbing quilt layer
   60/120mm load-bearing timbers at 625mm centres
   12/60mm firrings
   waterproof underlay
   19mm chipboard (v100G)
   220mm roof beams at 625mm centres
   120 + 100mm mineral fibre insulation
   vapour barrier
   24mm battens
   15mm gypsum fibreboard

2 wood shiplap boarding
   24mm battens
   polythene quilt
   16mm chipboard (v100G)
   140mm mineral fibre insulation
   60/140mm timber studding at 625mm centres
   polythene sheet vapour barrier
   15mm gypsum fibreboard

3 two-skin party wall between houses (cavity = 50mm)
   15mm gypsum fibreboard
   polythene sheet vapour barrier
   60/100mm timber studding at 625mm centres
   100 mm mineral fibre insulation
   12.5 + 10mm gypsum fibreboard

4 2 mm linoleum
   50mm cement and sand screed
   separating layer
   2 x 30mm foamed plastic insulating slabs
   bitumous waterproof sheeting
   concrete floor slab

1. Site plan.
2. View of the house at night.

dent.' The primary heavy-timber structure, made up of telephone poles, holds up the roof, while the 'stables' (kitchen and garage) and 'lofts' (bedrooms) to either side of the central 'threshing floor' (living room) are built of conventional platform-framed construction. Black steel 'jewellery' makes the structural connections. Quite clearly, however, this is no barn. The main elevation overlooking Bedford Basin has a modern and dynamic rhythm. Bay windows project on to a deck, while the windows of the upper floor pull back, retreating under the all-encompassing shingle-covered roof. Windows form into abstract patterns along the side walls. On the rear elevation, the staircase is expressed as an asymmetric element, bulging out of the main body of the building. Inside, instead of stalls and mangers there are living rooms and bedrooms. The double-height living room forms the heart of the tartan grid plan. To one side of this is the kitchen, with a dining area projecting from it. To the other is a study and garage. Upstairs, the house is symmetrical: two large bedrooms each with en-suite bathrooms and terraces, are separated by the void created by the double-height living room below. It is an ideal arrangement for a family with children, ensuring privacy and space for all. The plan will not necessarily remain like this, however. The intention, says MacKay-Lyons, is that the layout of the house should be sufficiently loose to be able to change over the years.

The material and building cultures on which Brian MacKay-Lyons draws are those of the forms and techniques of barn- and boat-building in Nova Scotia, where he was raised and where he now has his office. For centuries, the architecture of the region has been tied to the fishing and boat-building industries which once were the area's economic cornerstone. The same carpenters built boats, houses and other buildings in Halifax and its neighbouring towns and villages. The resulting architecture comprised simple and sparsely detailed 'stick frame' structures (with minimal openings on to the harsh outdoors) which were nevertheless strikingly bold in form and often brightly coloured. MacKay-Lyons' work is not nostalgic: although he works within the conventions of local construction methods, he does not try to mimic the local style. Instead, his understanding of these traditions allows him to move on to develop a new language that, while wholly contemporary, is also deeply connected to its context. MacKay-Lyons likens himself to a contemporary boat-builder. Like them, he says, he is 'not sentimental about the past, but pragmatic'. The LeGallais House is typical of MacKay-Lyons' work. Built of wood, like all his domestic buildings, the house is an abstraction of the vernacular barn. 'This black barn adheres to the strict spatial syntax of the Lunenburg [a local town] barn,' explains Mackay-Lyons. 'Its minimalist, contemporary detailing is consistent with the spartan ethic of its prece-

29

LeGallais House

Halifax, Nova Scotia,

Canada, 1992

Brian MacKay-Lyons

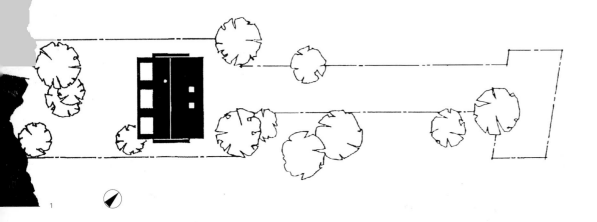

4

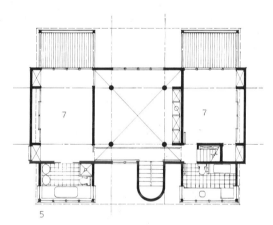

5

key

1 entry
2 kitchen
3 dining
4 living
5 study
6 garage
7 bedroom

LeGallais House

3. Inside, the primary heavy-timber structure is a dominant feature.
4. The ground floor is open plan.
5. First-floor plan.
6. Ground-floor plan.
7. The bathroom.

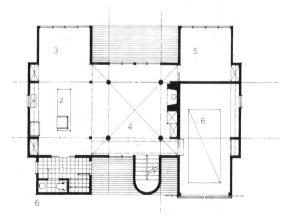

6

7

LeGallais House

8, 9 + 10. Construction details of the hearth and bookcase.

11. Close-up of the post-and-beam construction method, showing the cabinetry of natural maple and black lacquer.

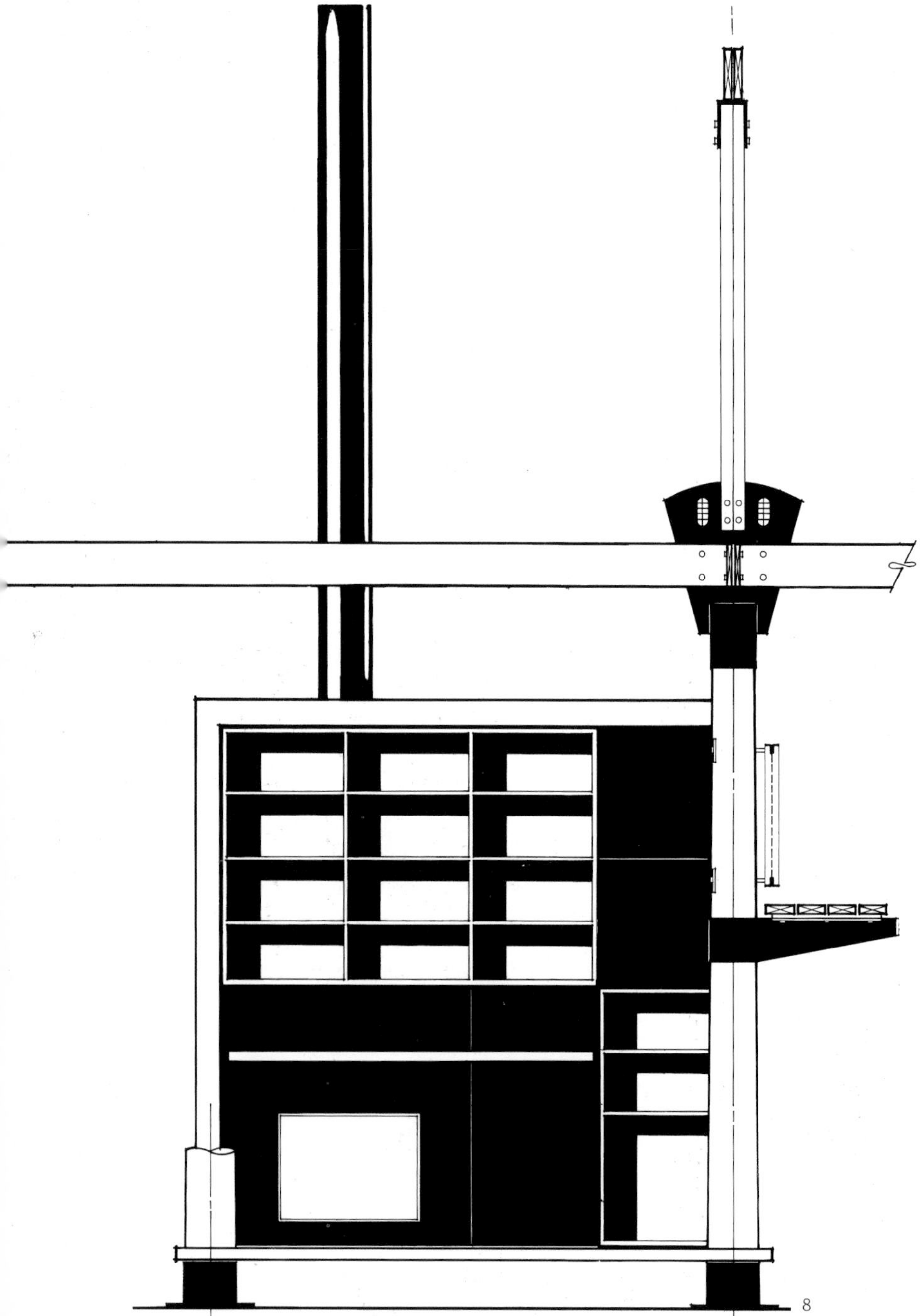

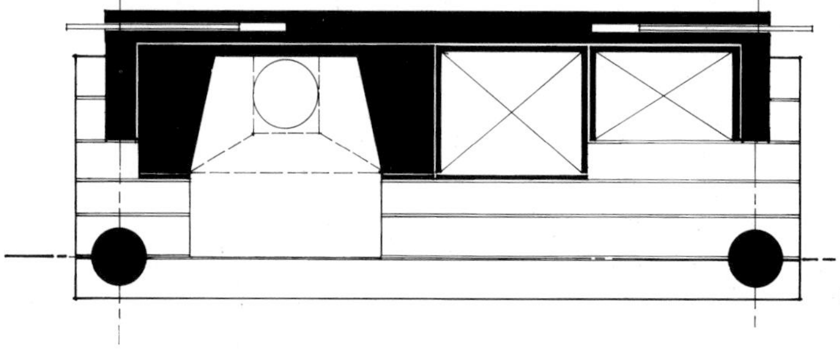

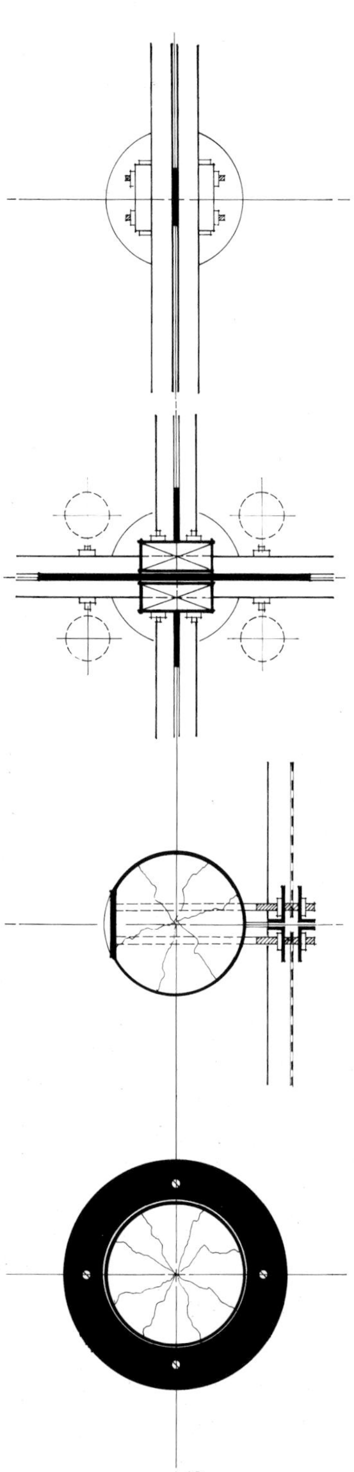

LeGallais House

Client: Susan and Brad LeGallais
Architect: Brian MacKay-Lyons
Architecture Urban Design
Project team: Brian MacKay-Lyons, Andrew King, Brenda Webster, Niall Savage
Structural engineer: Campbell Comeau Engineering
Builder: Gordon MacLean

1. Computer model of the pavilion.
2. Entrance.

overleaf
3. Front and side elevations.

20 years (the time it takes for the shrine's special construction techniques to be transmitted to the next generation, and the lifetime of the untreated wood), making it an appropriate source for a temporary structure. The shrine's formal severity also informed Ando's design. Where other Japanese architects draw on the tradition of the tea house, Ando sought to return to an earlier and more elemental style, epitomized by this sacred building. The pavilion had the shrine's forceful simplicity. The four-storey building was supported by a series of posts and beams made from Scandinavian and Canadian laminated pine. Inside, at fourth-floor level, the structure was visible, silhouetted against the translucent Teflon-coated fabric roof. Outside, the walls – clad in large lapped boards of laminated iroko – were curved in shape in accordance with the traditional concept of *sori*. Once inside – via a fearsomely steep arched bridge – visitors stepped literally from West to East. Passing under a pair of columns and a network of beams which stood like a symbolic tree, lit up by daylight but protecting those below its branch-like structure – visitors were drawn into the main gallery, a huge room more than 17 metres (56 feet) high, and then on into a sequence of galleries displaying aspects of Japanese history. After the pavilion was dismantled, its timber was sold for use in other buildings. It seems a fitting destiny for a building based on the forms and principles of the Ise Shrine.

'When I planned the Japanese Pavilion for the 1992 Exposition in Spain, a country with a tradition of building in stone, I resolved that the pavilion should not be a mere container for exhibits but rather that it should be in itself an expression of the culture of Japan,' explains Tadao Ando. 'In order to acquaint people with the culture of Japan, a land of wood, I considered that building the pavilion in wood was the best thing to do.' Since ancient times, Japanese architecture has been constructed out of timber. 'This culture of wood dwells within the spirit of the people of Japan and has become a key to understanding Japanese history and tradition,' says Ando. Timber is also quick to erect and dismantle, and relatively inexpensive. So when the Japanese government approached him to design its temporary pavilion at Expo '92, Ando forsook his more customary concrete and constructed his first timber building. At 60 metres (197 feet) long, 40 metres (130 feet) deep and 25 metres (82 feet) tall, the pavilion – which has since been dismantled – was one of the largest wooden structures in the world. Its scale was only made possible by the latest technology – computers, for example, played a large part in the pavilion's design, and all the wood is laminated – but the building's influences were visibly rooted in traditional Japanese architecture. Its primary reference was the Ise Shrine in central Japan. First constructed in the seventh century, this wooden structure is rebuilt every

30

Japanese Pavilion at

Expo '92

Seville, Spain, 1992

Tadao Ando Architect &

Associates

1

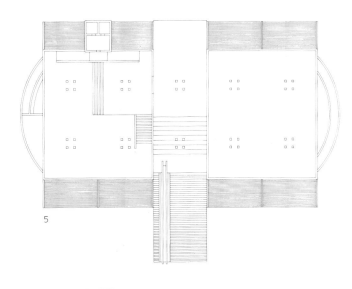

5

6

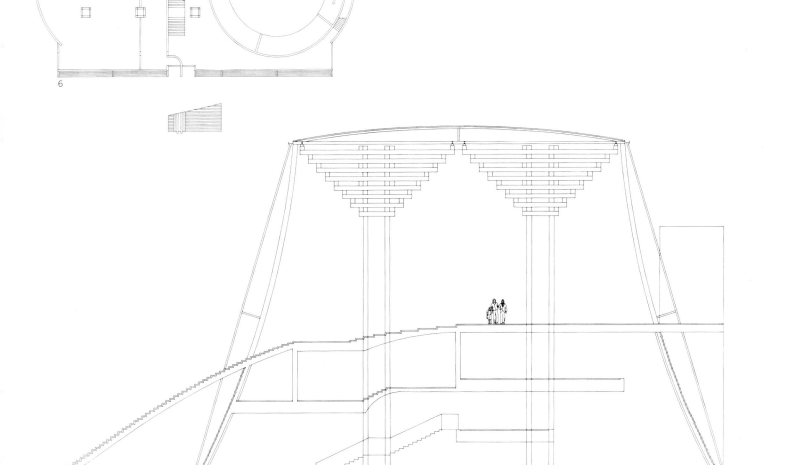

7

Japanese Pavilion at Expo '92
4. View up through one of the structural posts.
5. Entrance-level plan.
6. First-floor plan.
7. Cross-section through the pavilion.

Japanese Pavilion at Expo '92
Project team: Tadao Ando Architect & Associates

1. Possible front elevations.
2. The prototype house.

costs are thus reduced (construction costs work out at $35 per square foot, roughly half the typical cost in metropolitan Montreal). As with most Canadian houses it is 'stick built', made of a prefabricated frame of Canadian pine and erected on site. The homes went into full production in 1998. Buyers can participate in the design of the façades, choosing between a range of finishes (wood panels, brick, recycled or galvanized sidings), the size and types of windows, and the roofline (flat roof, mezzanine, attic space or cathedral ceiling). Internally, too, the design is sufficiently flexible for residents to dictate their own arrangements. Using a catalogue of options and computer visualizations, buyers can divide up the Next Home as they want. All three floors can be used as a family house. Alternatively, it can be divided up into a mix of single- or two-storey flats – ideal accommodation for the increasing number of people not living in traditional family structures. Buyers also get to decide on the internal organization of their units; they can determine room sizes and the positioning of the staircases. The narrowness of the house means that there is no internal support. Rooms can change as and when necessary, allowing for family expansion or contraction, or the need for a home office. The vernacular has always been adaptive, absorbing changes in social and economic structures. In this respect, the Next Home not only looks vernacular, but also takes forward a long and distinguished tradition.

The Next Home is a vernacular house with a difference. Its picket fence, gabled eaves and traditional looks belie the fact that it is a radical experiment in thinking about the house of the twenty-first century. The prototype house has been designed by the school of architecture at Canada's McGill University in Montreal, in association with a Quebecois building materials producer, a mortgage company and a housing corporation. This odd assortment of interest groups came together in response to the increasing 'affordability gap' in Montreal, due to house prices rising faster than incomes. The result, the Next Home, does more than merely provide low-cost accommodation; it also addresses changing patterns of use. 'New categories of first-time purchasers are entering the marketplace – such as couples without children or single parents – and we must meet their housing needs,' explains Avi Friedman, professor of architecture at McGill. 'The Next Home offers a glimpse of what homes will be like in the new millennium: streamlined, personalized, designed to change and priced for our challenging economic trends.' The house comes either detached, semi-detached or terraced. Despite adopting the forms of vernacular Montreal housing, with its slightly Gothic appearance, the Next Home is fundamentally different from traditional homes. The three-storey building is narrower than is customary, helping to reduce both the cost of land purchase, and the overall external elevation. Building

31

Next Home

Quebec, Canada, 1996

School of Architecture,

McGill University

1

2

3

4

5

Next Home
Architect: Dr Avi Friedman
Project team: Dr Avi Friedman,
Jasmin S. Frechette, Cyrus M. Bilimoria,
David Krawitz, Doug Raphael
Structural engineer: Daniel Boulanger
(Fermco Industries Ltd)

6

Index
Index of architects, designers and projects